Quality Time

Quality Time

Productivity Through Time Management

David D. Van Fleet

Arizona State University

INFORMATION AGE PUBLISHING, INC.
Charlotte, NC • www.infoagepub.com

Library of Congress Cataloging-in-Publication Data

A CIP record for this book is available from the Library of Congress
http://www.loc.gov

ISBN: 978-1-64802-241-8 (Paperback)
978-1-64802-242-5 (Hardcover)
978-1-64802-243-2 (E-Book)

Printed and bound by CPI Group (UK) Ltd, Croydon, CR0 4YY

This work is dedicated to my wife who has helped me manage my time in so many ways.

Contents

Preface

The overarching view in this book is that time itself is not what matters but rather how that time is used to achieve individual and organizational productivity goals. You plan your goals and how you will spend your time to achieve them. You assist others in planning their use of time. You organize your and others' activities so as to make the best use of everyone's time. You strive to control extraneous factors that would impede the best use of everyone's time. And, of course, you lead through example by properly managing your own use of time.

Managers and their team members typically wake up every morning, send their children to school, kiss their spouses goodbye, rush to work, and don't return home until 7:00 p.m. So, half their day is spent focused on work. Thus, it is extremely important that their time at work be used to the best result possible so as not to deplete self and family time further. Managers and non-managers are accustomed to this sort of routine and seldom consider how better use of their time would benefit not just their organizations but also themselves and quite possibly their friends and families as well. This book is designed to help them do just that.

Books, articles, workshops, seminars, and the like proffer general advice on time management. Most of that advice is specifically targeted to individuals, without consideration of how one person can help another to plan for better use of time. Seldom is counsel provided to groups or teams for managing time that involves interactions among team members that affect their use of time. This book fills that need. It is the first to offer both

Quality Time, pages xi–xiii

general and specific information and advice from both an individual and a team or group point of view. It is designed so that you are involved first. Then you involve members of your group or team to also take action. Reciprocal communication enables all parties to become productive through better use of time.

Managers who get upset over employees coming to work late or socializing on the job appear to care more about them "putting in time" than putting their time to good use. Managers who focus solely on time usually concentrate on the wrong things. They're saying being on the job is important when they should be saying that what's really important is what is accomplished on the job. The approach in this book will be to focus on the use of time to achieve goals or objectives. In other words, *time itself is not what matters but rather how that time is used to achieve individual and organizational productivity goals.*

Standards

This book follows six standards: readable, interesting, up-to-date, accurate, unique, and audience. The first two assure that the book is readily understandable by a diverse audience while others assure that it is of high quality and targeted to those most likely to need it.

Readable

To ensure readability *Quality Time* avoids unnecessary jargon and summaries of research. The use of straightforward language that involves the reader and a logical sequencing of material contribute to making the material clear and understandable to you the reader.

Interesting

Quality Time tries to make learning easier and more enjoyable by making the material realistic and more interesting. Assessments and a variety of "tools" are provided to make applications of the material relevant and understandable to you and your group or team.

Up To Date

To be on the cutting edge means to have the most up-to-date material available. *Quality Time* is current and timely in its content.

Accurate

Quality Time is firmly grounded in research but not burdened with unnecessary references although numerous sources are provided. Careful use of research assures that the material is accurate, while practical examples assure that it is relevant.

Unique

Quality Time is different from other self-help time-management books. Most others are focused on only the individual reader. *Quality Time* is intended to serve both managers and members of the work team. It recognizes that achieving productivity through managing organization time requires back-and-forth problem solving by everyone in the organization.

Audience

Quality Time was written primarily for employees, especially managers, in all types of business and government organizations, including schools, universities, law enforcement, healthcare, real estate, finance, and the fire service. While focused on managers, the unique framework and assessments are valuable to anyone. It is written at a level that is appropriate for individuals in either self-study, training, or classroom settings. The reader needs no special business, organizational, or technical background to understand this book. The more experience in organizations that the reader has, however, the more the reader will recognize the value of the material; but the less experience that the reader has, the more he or she probably needs the information presented in the book.

Acknowledgments

The philosophy underlying *Quality Time* owes a debt to the work of Flint (2018) and Morrison (2017). Their concepts guided the development of this unique approach to time management from a group or team perspective. Although some of the tools found in *Quality Time* are similar to those in Griffin and Van Fleet (2013, Chapter 3), they have been modified and expanded and the approach using those tools in a group setting is unique. The author also especially thanks Dr. Ella W. Van Fleet for her insightful comments and suggestions on earlier drafts. Her suggestions and encouragement were central to the completion of this work.

Quality Time, page xv

1

Quality Time

Nothing is a waste of time if you use the experience wisely.
—Rodin

Time itself is not what matters but rather how that time is used to achieve individual and organizational productivity goals. Managers who get upset over employees coming to work late or socializing on the job often care more about them "putting in time" than putting their time to good use. Managers who focus solely on time concentrate on the wrong things (Van Fleet, 1982, 1986). They're saying that being on the job is important when they should be saying that what's accomplished on the job is what is really important. Time used effectively and efficiently in the pursuit of both personal and organizational productivity is *quality time.* This book is designed to help you and your group or team achieve quality time. While it is focused on managers, the unique framework and assessments are valuable and useful to any individual in an organization.

Quality Time, pages 1–5

Managers May Emphasize Wrong Thing

What some managers would consider a waste of time actually could be a constructive part of an employee's day. For example, individuals sitting around and talking on the job may appear to be wasting company time, but through that sort of social interaction employees can develop healthy relationships—the trust and sense of closeness necessary for getting along when they're working as a team. People are, after all, social by nature; so, by working together, they use each other's unique strengths and abilities to accomplish more than if they just worked alone.

Remember, though, that while *quality time* is suitable for all jobs, some of the specifics in this book may not apply to jobs where opening dates or times are rigidly maintained. In a school, retail operation, bank, or assembly line work where interdependencies exist, for example, obviously the employee needs to be there to do his or her job before others can do theirs.

Emphasize Performance, Not Time

Although time is important in all jobs, there are a tremendous number of jobs where performance and productivity, not time, should be emphasized. *Employees should be rewarded for what they do, not for how much time they take in doing it.* Many assembly-line or other factory jobs actually reflect both the amount of time worked and the quantity of work produced.

Individual Accomplishments Not Equal

One of the difficulties with payment for work time rather than productivity is that it assumes that if employees are present for 8 hours, they will simply work at a pace that accomplishes a certain amount of work in those 8 hours. The reality is that if workers were allowed some flexibility, a little more freedom, to come and go, they might accomplish the same but take only 7.5 hours. Regrettably, some managers may say, "You owe us that half-hour," when that is simply not the case. If given the flexibility, a worker is far more likely to develop an appreciation for the organization, loyalty to the manager, and a lasting dedication to the company to deal with emergency circumstances. *People should be hired to accomplish things, not put in time.*

If you were to say to a college athlete "When we say lights out at 8:00 p.m., we mean literally 8:00 p.m. and it can't be 5 minutes later." They would find that ridiculous and oppressive. But the same thing is true of a 40 or 50-year-old employee. You're talking about a mature adult and to say to them that it really makes a difference whether they're off 5 minutes or so one way or another, they know that's not really the case.

Now if you're talking about 30 minutes late or 2 hours late, that's another story. But most of the "time theft" advocates deal with these little 1- or 2- or 3-minute things. When two employees go to the break room and become engaged in conversation about the weather or politics or something, they are building relationships and loyalty to the organization. In the short term, they may appear to be spending 5 or 10 minutes more than they should and some might say that it's wasted time, but it may not be wasted. At some point, the organization will need them to work together and the fact that they know each other and can talk to each other will make their performances that much better and their loyalty to the organization stronger. If they are "time thieves," spending too much time on what some might consider wasted time, you will know this by their unsatisfactory performance.

Sustaining High Performance Time

Managers must take burnout into account. When you ask people if they can accomplish more on their jobs, they'll probably say, "yes." But when you ask them how long they could sustain that level, it's a whole new ball game. Some could manage it for only a short time while others perhaps a bit longer, but there are limits for everyone. Managers must take the possibility of burnout into account when setting performance expectations for others.

Cause and Effect

Managers who blame lagging productivity on employees wasting time are usually at fault for being poor examples or misdirecting activities. They focus on effects instead of causes. It's like mopping up water that's dripping on the floor without ever worrying about where it's coming from. The emphasis should be on performance.

Rewarding Individual Performance

Managers who want better results from their group or team members may need to change the reward system, both tangible and intangible. They should take into account that different people work at different paces and those who finish first usually feel that they deserve a reward of a longer break. Rewards should be linked to performance or goal accomplishment rather than time. Some people don't have to apply themselves as hard as others to accomplish their goals.

Time, Culture, and the Reward System

One reason why managers emphasize time is that it is easier to measure time than results, especially in groups. Individual effort is not sufficient. Individuals working together can accomplish more than the sum of their individual efforts. The key is developing groups or teams so that they use their time to contribute to the value of the organization. To assure that your group or team is contributing to the value of the organization, you need to create a culture—an atmosphere—in which people accomplish their goals and those of the organization and like doing it. True, stress is involved, but mostly enjoyable stress. There is pressure to perform, but they have expectations that good performance will be rewarded. Developing performance norms focused on goal attainment rather than exclusively time norms is called for. The idea is "let's get the job done, let's work together" rather than "Me boss, you worker." It should be "We're all part of the same team trying to get the job done. If it takes 7 hours, fine; if it takes 9 hours, so be it. Let's just get the job done and get it done right."

While this situation may sound like a pleasant atmosphere in which to work, it may not be; because where the emphasis is truly on achieving performance goals, there can be a lot of stress which could only be made worse if there is also stress related to time (see Chapter 7, "Time and Stress"). Employees do what they perceive as necessary to get rewards. Managers should concentrate on rewarding the achievement of performance goals rather than worrying about the detailed use of time.

This is true of every level of management. All of us can make better use of our time by understanding the role that time plays in organizations. Your organization's value in the marketplace depends on time—products being delivered on time, customer's inquiries being promptly handled, employees being at work on time, everyone using his or her time to greatest effect. You as a manager play a significant role in ensuring that all members of your unit, group, or team are using their time to contribute to the organization's value. It all comes down to one final question: Is everyone, including you, using his or her time in such a way as to assure the continuance of your organization's value? Does everyone understand that *it's not the time that counts but rather how the time is used?*

With a boss who is obsessed with time rather than performance, it may be easier just to make the boss happy by coming to work on time, taking it easy all day long, then leaving promptly at 5:00 as though you have had a productive day and finished your work on time. In many organizations, employees put in far more hours than they would if their manager does not insist on clocking in at 8 and out at 5. They put in more time because they are trying to get to a particular level of accomplishment. *It is easier to be punctual than it is to achieve high performance results.*

Your goal is to achieve quality time. As noted earlier, quality time is time used effectively and efficiently in the pursuit of both personal and organizational productivity goals. With the help of the ideas in this book, you and your group or team should be able to achieve quality time.

Quality Time Questions

1. What is "productivity" in your organization?
2. Would the concept of quality time be appropriate for your organization?
3. What are the typical work hours in your organization? In your particular unit?
4. In what way does the reward system use time as a component?

Quality Time Actions

Discuss each of these concepts with your subordinates or team members to be sure everyone understands each of them.

2

V-REEL

A New Way

It's not enough to be busy, so are the ants. The question is, what are we busy about?
—Henry David Thoreau

Understanding how to achieve *quality time* in organizational groups and teams is vital to the success of those organizations. Yet all too frequently time is not handled well and so it is not quality time. Managing time is usually seen as personal, not something you as a manager can regulate. One person staring off into space is thinking about how best to do something while another person is only daydreaming.

As you look around at other people in your organization, do you think that your peers and/or team members sometimes seem to operate without goals, without any clear direction, without a clear understanding of their role in creating and maintaining the value of the organization? If they had a clear understanding of their roles in creating the organization's value and goals associated with that creation, they would be more likely to use their

Quality Time, pages 7–15

time wisely and achieve quality time. To achieve that understanding, you and your team need a new way of thinking about how time is used in your organization.

The concept of V-REEL®, originally developed to improve strategic thinking in organizations, provides that new way (Flint, 2018). As used here, it is a framework that provides a unique way of thinking about the use of time. V-REEL consists of five components—value, rareness, eroding factors, enabling factors, and longevity.

Value, as used here, does not refer to a company's market value as determined by its market capitalization. Nor does it refer to the intangible value derived from patents, trademarks, or the like. Intangible value may be estimated by determining the worth of both debt and equity of the organization and then subtracting the value of all tangible assets. Instead, value can be seen in terms of importance or significance to customers. It can result from the usefulness of the organization's productivity or output. Adopting the approach of Flint (2018), value is the customer's perception "that a product, service, or experience is worth more than the money it costs to create" (p. 166). Using the concept of V-REEL, we would try to ascertain how your time and that of others contribute to the organization's value?

Rareness refers to the capability of managing time within the firm or its competitive cohort (for more on the competitive cohort see Flint & Van Fleet, 2011). Clearly, some groups or teams have a greater possibility of managing their time than do others. Do you or your group have any distinctive competencies (assets or resources) that are "rare," that are unique so that others may not also have them? You would want to build on and protect these as they are vital to achieving quality time. So, it is important to recognize just how much control over time the group has.

Eroding factors are those things that impede your use of time or your ability to manage your own time. They get in the way of achieving quality time. Unexpected interruptions are clearly eroding factors.

Enabling factors are those things that improve your use of time or your ability to manage it. They help you to achieve quality time. Learning new skills or adopting time-saving products could well be an enabling factor.

Finally, *longevity* suggests how long any given measure of time management might be sustained. Will your efforts be short-lived, or will they continue for quite a while? Immediate "fixes" in a group's use of time may well be short-lived but changes to the group's culture regarding the use of time are more likely to last.

The V-REEL framework is not a quick fix, but its use can aid you and your group or team in achieving and maintaining quality time. You and your group or team need to have clear goals that are linked to the value of your organization. You and they should identify eroding factors and consider how to reduce their impact. Likewise enabling factors should be identified and efforts made to take advantage of them. This new way of thinking about the use of time is useful to you as an individual but also very useful in a group or team setting. Fully utilizing it will not be quick nor easy but doing so will result in a strong culture and the achievement of quality time.

Background

To appreciate this new way of thinking about your use of time and that of others and to develop your understanding of organization time, some basic background concepts need to be clarified.

Goals

Goals refer to desired states or conditions that are being sought. Goals should provide a clear purpose or direction. Goals may be called missions, purposes, goals, objectives, ends, and aims. When considering organization time, goals refer to desired individual or group outcomes. Thus, they should be relatively specific, have clear time frames, and be measurable to some degree. Importantly, these individual and group goals should clearly support the organization's value. Individuals have multiple goals, some more personal, others organizational, so it is important that priorities be established for those goals.

Priority refers to the importance in accomplishing longer-term goals—just because something is due "tomorrow" does not mean that it is a priority item. Potential conflicts between long-term personal and organizational goals must be resolved. Managers can play an important role in assisting members of their group in that regard.

> Mary seems to never get things done. She lists things to be done but seems unable to carry them out. One reason may be that she has too many "to-do" lists—on her cell phone, her computer, a calendar at her desk—and she gets them confused. She says that she needs more time or more information or more help. As a result, others are having to pick up the slack to see to it that things do get done.

Mary doesn't really understand goals. *To be sure that your team doesn't have any Marys in it, you need to have clear goals; you need to engage in open and honest communication.*

> Yogi Berra purportedly said, "If you don't know where you are going, you'll end up someplace else." The exchange between Alice and the Cheshire Cat in Lewis Carroll's work is often paraphrased as *"If you don't know where you're going, any road will get you there." You need goals.*

Group Versus Team

In common parlance, a group consists of individuals working more or less independently of one another whereas a team is a group that shares a common purpose. Formally, work teams and groups: (a) consist of two or more individuals, (b) exist to perform organizationally relevant tasks, (c) share one or more goals, (d) interact socially, (e) exhibit task interdependencies (such as workflow, goals, or outcomes), (f) maintain and manage boundaries, and (g) are in an organization that sets boundaries and constraints (Kozlowski & Bell, 2003). Thus, the primary distinction between a group and a team revolves around the extent or degree of interdependencies that exist in the group. If interdependence is relatively low, it is commonly referred to as a group; if interdependence is relatively high, it is referred to as a team. Teams are the concern in this book.

In most organizations, all groups share the overall purpose of the organization and are, then, "on the same team." Hopefully, everyone in the group or team is committed to both individual and organizational goals. With the goal as the unifying characteristic, teams can get results more quickly and with more creativity. But the manager is vital in providing leadership and to assure open communication, free expression, trust, flexibility, and consensus. The manager must make a conscious effort to mediate conflicts before they become eroding factors and to keep the group's or team's "eyes on the prize" as enabling factors. Thus, the term team will be used here to refer to any and all groups within an organization focused on achieving value for the organization.

Teams, then, come in a variety of sizes and types and may be called departments, committees, task forces, self-managed teams, project teams, boards, or even juries. These groups or teams may be more prevalent in flatter organizational structures, when flexible hours or job sharing is used, or even for those working at home via a computer.

Free Riding

When a member of a group or team who obtains benefits from the group or team but does not share his or her share of the costs (the work itself) of providing the benefits, it is called *free riding* (Albanese & Van Fleet, 1985a, 1985b). Free riding, however, is not necessarily free loading. The theory underlying this concept is concerned primarily with the provision of public goods by large groups. Teams usually do not consist of a large group and so the concept doesn't fit very well. Nevertheless, while it is seldom the case in organizations that "pure" free riders exist, there are no doubt instances where a group or team member is perceived as not carrying his or her weight and this would be an eroding factor for the team.

The use of appropriate inducements can be enabling factors. Those inducements could be financial incentives or special forms of recognition to particular group members that may help to alleviate any free riding. Having clearly identifiable goals is also enabling and can help to identify when or if a team member seems to be slacking but the best way to counter this issue is through the development of a strong organizational culture focused on creating value for the organization.

Also, strong organizational cultures can elicit an enthusiastic commitment to the purposes and tasks of the organization and that means that team members, when they decide how to use their time, will place a commitment to the organization as a behavioral norm. The satisfaction they receive from being a team member in such a culture serves as a special incentive that encourages their contribution to the organization's goals.

Participation and Delegation

Their role also can be enhanced through the use of participation. *Participation* is an enabling factor and refers to the extent to which a manager allows group members to take part in decisions that affect them. If group members want to take part, managers need to consider allowing them to do so. Its members have no desire to participate, managers may use participation anyway to expand the horizon and capabilities of group members (essentially training). Participation can frequently lead to increased motivation among those involved as they experience increased feelings of responsibility and ownership of work. The manager needs to evaluate how much participation is merited in each situation. In some cases, a team member will be enabled to actually take charge of an activity by having it delegated to them.

Delegation refers to the process in which a manager assigns a portion of his or her task to an individual group member. Effective communication clarifies these relationships and assures that all members of the organization understand who is to do what and when as well as who is to work with and communicate with whom. This clarification is termed delegation. To be effective, delegation involves three steps—(a) assigning responsibility, (b) empowering the individual, and (c) creating accountability.

Assigning responsibility involves specifying the tasks to be performed and the time and quality expected. *Empowering the individual* involves granting that person the authority necessary to accomplish the tasks. *Creating accountability* identifies the obligation of the individual to perform the tasks. Time pressure on a manager should never be a reason to delegate as it could lead to lower levels of performance by turning over a task to someone not well prepared to do it. When group members are capable, they should be assigned the tasks, thus freeing the manager's time to concentrate on other matters. Likewise, when a manager feels confident that the group member could learn to perform the task, delegation to save time is in order.

Efficiency and Effectiveness

To appreciate the role of quality time in organizations, you must also understand the concepts of efficiency and effectiveness. Successful management involves achieving both efficiency and effectiveness. *Efficiency* means operating such that resources are not wasted. It is the ratio of output(s) to input(s). It is the relative results obtained or derived from resources, including time and effort, used or expended. Allowing surplus funds to sit idly in a bank account drawing little interest, having people do nothing while waiting for new work, generating large amounts of waste by-products from a poorly designed production system, paying people to work overtime to accomplish what should have been done during the normal work period, and acquiring but not using valuable information are examples of inefficiency. Note that inefficiency can relate to any category of resources. One key to successful management is to avoid this kind of situation. Successful managers will also be effective.

Effectiveness, on the other hand, is the degree to which an individual, group, or organization accomplishes or progresses toward the accomplishment of objectives or goals. It is not just getting things done, rather it is getting the right things done in the right way at the right times. Effectiveness means contributing to the organization's value. A manager who enters a new market just before it starts expanding, gets out of a market before it collapses, and maintains an appropriate competitive posture is more effective than one who enters a market as it starts to decline, gets out of a market just before it starts growing, and does not maintain an appropriate competitive posture. Effectiveness combined with efficiency is successful management. But as noted earlier, the sorts of environments described above involve stress.

Stress

Stress is common in organizations and life itself (see Chapter 9). Time or lack thereof can be a causal element in work stress so properly managing one's time is a useful technique for reducing stress. Stress refers to an individual's response to a strong stimulus called a stressor. The organization's culture can add to or diminish stress.

Stress generally follows a cycle referred to as the General Adaptation Syndrome or GAS. When an individual first encounters a stressor, the first stage, *alarm*, is activated. Initially, the individual may feel panic, wonder how to cope, and feel helpless. But after a short period of alarm, the individual gathers some strength and starts to resist the negative effects of the stressor. This is the second stage, *resistance*. In many cases, the resistance phase may end the GAS. If it does not end, prolonged exposure without resolution may bring on Stage 3, *exhaustion*. At this stage, the individual literally gives up. The consequences at this stage are eroding and are never good for the individual or the organization.

However, not all stress is bad. Without some level of stress, individuals become lethargic and don't do much of anything. An optimal level of stress, on the other hand, can be enabling and result in motivation and excitement. So, the key is determining when stress is too little or too great. Typically, in organizations, stress levels tend to be high so reductions in stressors are generally in order, particularly if the stress results from time pressure. Having clear, understandable, and achievable goals helps to alleviate stress.

Communication

Communication is the process of transmitting information and is an important enabling factor. It can be seen as the "glue" that binds components of an organization together, as both a one-way and a two-way process, as the means for coordinating activities in organizations, and as shared meaning between individuals. When considering organization time, it is important to recognize the pervasiveness of communication in the manager's job and to focus on communication between and among people—interpersonal communication. Thus, communication can take place within an organization between organizational units, between organizations, and even between governments. Adopting the approach of Morrison (2017, pp. 26–27), a clear and important task for managers is to communicate widely so as to assure that their subordinates and team members have clear, attainable goals that are linked to the organization's value. You need to balance your time demands with those of your group. Having open, honest communication about those time demands will lead to a better balance of everyone's use of time. This sort of communication is enabling and is an important step to creating a strong, positive culture for your team.

Culture

Finally, *culture* refers to the set of ideals that helps organization members understand what the organization stands for, how it does things, and what it considers important. Culture is a nebulous concept and can't be measured or directly observed. Nevertheless, because it is foundational to the organization, it plays a major role in shaping how time is used in the creation of the value of the organization. Having a diverse workforce can be enabling by increasing creativity and innovation to make better use of time as well as providing social support, but diversity can also increase tension and stress.

Adopting the approach of Morrison (2017, p. 45), managers should strive to create a culture of worth by recognizing the contributions of others and sending a clear message that management values its people. Further, managers should make the organization's culture one of hope by trusting employees and avoiding using fear in misguided motivation attempts (Morrison, 2017, p. 63). In this way, a strong culture that supports the value of the organization can be created. But occasionally some team members may not seem to be fully engaged. As noted earlier, they may be free riding. Clearly, you as a manager of a group or team have a vital role to play in how they use their time to contribute to the value of the organization. But just as the above concepts need to be clearly understood, so too, your role as a manager must be understood.

The next chapter suggests ways in which this new way of thinking could be applied.

A New Way Questions

1. How much attention have you been paying to productivity?
2. How much to time used productively?
3. What type of culture exists in your organization? In your particular unit?
4. What is your organization's value?

A New Way Actions

Discuss each of these concepts with your subordinates or team members to be sure everyone understands each of them. Focus particular attention on the V-REEL framework as it may be difficult to fully understand at this stage. However, as it is applied in the following sections of the book, you and your team will come to appreciate its usefulness.

3

Applying the New Way

Whether it's the best of times or the worst of times, it's the only time we've got.
—Art Buchwald

To help you better understand the V-REEL® concept as it can be applied to help you and/or your team achieve *quality time*, consider some examples of how it might be used.

Too Much or Too Little Time

Do you think that your team never has enough time to be productive and meet their goals? It might involve an eroding factor if the goal structure is inappropriate or if they don't really understand it. Or conversely, do they seem to have time on their hands—too much free time? Free time as they wait for others to get things done or tasks not properly sequenced? Do some seem to have a lot of free time while others don't? Maybe they haven't planned anything, including their day-to-day activities. Clearly, personal

Quality Time, pages 17–21

planning is an enabling factor and could help them use their time wisely but understanding the role of the team and its contribution to the organization's value is even more important.

> In an effort to save time, Lydia regularly writes emails while she chats on the phone to her clients. She thinks that this is a good use of her time, but the result is that she does both tasks poorly—her emails contain errors, and her clients are frustrated by her lack of concentration since they frequently have to ask her the same question more than once.

Lydia thinks she is saving time by multitasking but her poor results suggest that when you add in the time it takes to correct her errors, she is wasting time.

Lack of Involvement

Perhaps you note that no one seems to really communicate about what's going on. They seem reluctant to coordinate their activities, to assist one another, to engage others in tasks. This would especially be true of managers who fail to delegate. Failure to delegate would be an eroding factor. Participation and group involvement aren't being employed to accomplish goals. Communication, delegation, participation, and other forms of involvement all could be enabling factors to help everyone use their time more wisely, especially when those facilitate better use of time by everyone.

Improper Use of Goals

Bad managers have been known to use meetings as dreadful "show and tell" sessions. Tension is high when group meetings are held to ridicule those who failed to meet goals, to intimidate by pointing out individuals' errors, or to humiliate individuals or groups who missed their goals. Clearly, a better use of everyone's time would be to focus on improvement rather than embarrassment or punishment.

Poor Culture

Some organizations have a culture that results in clashes regarding production decisions. Senior managers argue passionately and uncensored regarding production issues, while the rest of the group and the production operators observe the exchange.

> Floyd lays out a specific plan to sell 100 motors at $1,000—10 in Quarter 1, 15 in Quarter 2, 25 in Quarter 3, and 50 in Quarter 4. Shane, on the other hand, suggests a more flexible approach to sell 70–100 motors at $750–$1,000 during the next year. They argue about their different approaches incessantly.

The behavior of the managers could carry into conference room discussions where a resolution is typically gained only when one point of view will eventually give way. The loss of productive time during these exchanges could be avoided if everyone recognized this sort of behavior as an eroding factor.

Stress and Inefficiency

In order to complete assignments, some employees are working long hours. Long hours that are constant or sustained for extended periods of time are stressful and inefficient. They can lead to fatigue, poor decision-making, slowed reflexes, muddled thinking, accidents, resentment against the company, and less than optimum performance. These consequences can be disastrous and almost always lead to decrements in health and productivity, or to high turnover. Perhaps restructuring the assignments or rescheduling assignments to better balance the workload is in order.

Failure to Use Time Wisely

But what about you? You can't expect others, particularly subordinates or team members, to use their time wisely unless you are first using yours wisely. So, think about your situation. Do you really understand your organization's value in the marketplace? Are you clear as to your goal and its connection to the organization's purpose? Lack of clear goals would be an eroding factor. You are more likely to use your time wisely if you have a clear understanding of your organization's value and how your goals link to that value. Such an understanding would be an enabling factor. But you also share in your team's goals and use of time. You need to understand your personal eroding and enabling factors to better assist you in helping your group or team with theirs.

> Vincent seems to get a rush from being busy. He narrowly meets deadlines, responds to every single email, has piles of files on his desk that he constantly rearranges to "make progress on," and he practically runs to any and all meetings. He seems to love the adrenaline buzz from his "addiction to busyness."

Vincent clearly does not use his time wisely. He's busy but seldom makes a real contribution to the organization's value.

Failure to Plan

Have you established plans for how you will be productive and accomplish your goals? Not just long-term plans, but also day-to-day ones. And have you done that for your team as well? Do you have sufficient time to get everything done or are you too often pressed for time? Because you have idle time as you wait for others, do you think that it will be quicker to do things yourself than to try to explain to others how things should be done? Thinking through these questions will assist you in identifying eroding and enabling factors impacting the use of time. Taking a longer time perspective would indicate that helping others by explaining the plan will lead to better use of time in the future.

> He's unbelievable! No wonder Harry can't get anything done; he says "yes" to every request that comes along. So not only is he overworking himself, but people take advantage of his good nature to "dump" all sorts of stuff on him.

Harry clearly has no clear-cut goals and plans for how to achieve them. Saying "yes" is an eroding factor for Harry while personal planning would be an enabling factor.

Reluctance to Delegate

Perhaps you are reluctant to delegate to others or use participative management because you think that if you really want it done right, you need to do it yourself. Yet, involving others would clearly ease any time pressures that you feel. True, in some instances it may feel that more time is required to show someone else how to do something than to do the work yourself. The more hours you work, it may seem, the more you have to do ["The harder I work, the behinder I get!"].

> I tried delegating an assignment once but was pretty unhappy with the way it turned out. I kept checking to see how it was going, but it seemed that the more I got involved, the further behind the assignment was. It finally got finished but took longer than it would have if I'd done it myself and probably not as good either. So now I don't delegate because I want to be sure that things are done right. Besides none of my subordinates have the background and experience that I have.

If this sounds familiar, then you need to more fully understand the role of time and how it relates to the value of your organization. Failing to delegate is an eroding factor while appropriate delegations are enabling factors. You should now see that everyone's time is important, and it must begin with you. The next chapters will help you determine just how you are currently using your time.

Applying the New Way Questions

1. Do any of the examples in this chapter apply to your situation?
2. How do you anticipate making changes?

Applying the New Way Actions

As you attempt to apply the V-REEL framework to achieve quality time, consider the impact on not just you but also members of your group or team.

4

Management and Managers

If you want to make good use of your time, you've got to know what's most important and then give it all you've got.

—Lee Iacocca

You don't have to have a title to be a manager and you don't have to be a manager to benefit from focusing on quality time. To be sure that everyone is "on the same page," being clear as to what is meant by management and managers is necessary. Those who are usually thought of as managers include owners and operators of organizations, small or large such as retailing, manufacturing, and service firms; governments at all levels; professional sports organizations; and the like are all managers. They may be called an officer, an executive, a manager, a supervisor, a foreman, a leadman, some other title, or no title at all.

Quality Time, pages 23–28

What Is a Manager

Whether or not you have a title, you are a manager when you deal with activities within the organization and you are accountable for your role in maintaining the organization's value. And your role includes the performance of your group or team. Even if you are not a manager, you need to come to a better appreciation of the nature of the managerial task and organization time. That will assist you in assuring that you and your group or team develop *quality time* to contribute to the value of the organization whatever type of organization it is.

Management is complex.

What Is Management

Each type of organization and the people who manage them suggest that management is complex. Managers handle numerous different activities and those activities change frequently. Typically, organizations begin with a founder, an entrepreneur, who has a vision of the organization's value in the marketplace. As the organization grows and evolves, others are brought in to assist and goals based on maintaining that value are established. As the organization develops, changes occur, and new members, managers, and workers may not have a clear understanding of the organization's value in the marketplace. One major challenge managers face is to keep the overall value of the organization clear and current. But all too frequently day-to-day functions impede meeting that challenge.

Traditionally, management was thought to be limited to one particular set of people in an organization who were called managers. Today management is seen as a set of activities that must be performed for an organization to be successful. That set of activities could be concentrated in a few people or dispersed over many people. Highly successful organizations seem to have everyone involved in management although certain individuals will focus their attention more tightly on selected aspects while others will focus on other aspects or even on nonmanagerial activities of the organization. Since everyone is involved in management, everyone is actually a manager to at least some degree. The term manager is used to refer to those whose activities are more focused on managerial than nonmanagerial activities and who have individuals reporting to them. Even so, everything discussed here applies to everyone in an organization.

Management involves coordination and can be defined as a set of activities directed at the efficient and effective utilization of resources in the pursuit of one or more goals. Everyone is involved, some more so than others, in shaping internal organizational environments and cultures in such a way that the organization's value in the marketplace is understood and everyone becomes committed to attaining and sustaining that value. In a well-managed organization, then, participants perform well because they want to and enjoy doing so.

> By the time I get through all of my emails and phone messages, half the day is gone. I can't seem to get ahead of my tasks because I have to spend so much time with these so-called "time-saving" devices! I think that I'd be better off if I got rid of email and my answering machine. Then maybe I'd get some work done.

Emails and phone calls are a part of management. Management is an extremely complex process. Part of this complexity stems from the different activities in which managers are engaged. It is not a cerebral activity limited to sitting around thinking. Management involves action. Managers are constantly engaged in talking, listening, reading, writing, meeting, observing, and participating. Managers talk with other managers, their subordinates, individuals outside the organization. They use telephones and computers. They attend meetings and oversee meetings. They fill in forms and write memos and reports. They are just simply busy. The complexity of managerial activity continually serves as a source of new excitement, and its diversity is a reward for those seeking new challenges. It requires a lot of energy and has many rewards. Another characteristic of managerial activity is its pervasiveness—it is everywhere. Management is not limited to businesses. It is also practiced in universities, government agencies, health care organizations, social organizations, and families. Indeed, management can be found in virtually every collection of people who find it necessary to coordinate their activities. Thus, it is well worth developing a better understanding of how these organizations function and how time is managed in them.

Management also involves the use of resources. These may be human resources (hourly, salary—everyone in the organization), physical resources (buildings, office furniture, and raw materials), financial resources (retained earnings, product sales, and bank loans), and informational resources (sales projections and market research). Management serves to help the organization create and maintain value in the marketplace. It does so through the accomplishment of appropriate goals. Goals are targets for organizations. Setting appropriate goals is critical to an organization maintaining its value. How time is used by an organization's human resources in pursuit of those goals is critical to the accomplishment of the organization's value.

What Managers Do

A common way of classifying managerial activity is by its role in the organization: strategic, advisory or informational, and operational. The dividing lines are arbitrary, but strategic management refers to setting overall organizational goals, determining strategy and operating policies, and representing the organization to the external environment. The heads of organizations engage in primarily strategic management activities and are usually called strategic managers or executives. Strategic managers' jobs are demanding, and turnover is common. Most managerial activity is advisory or informational management activity. People who engage in these activities more than any other have titles like plant manager, division manager, and operations manager.

Although these positions are changing and some experts warn that many of them may disappear in the future, these managers generally facilitate the implementation of the strategies and policies by providing information and expertise to others. Operational managers are those who carry out the day-to-day managerial activities of the organization. They are called supervisors, foreman, and coordinators. As is the case with advisory managers, the job of the operational manager is changing dramatically. But whatever label is used, this book is for you.

Management also involves certain functions. Those managerial functions can be classified as planning, organizing, controlling, and leading, each of which involves time.

Planning your use of time and that of your group or team involves decision-making, and problem-solving to determine appropriate goals and how best to achieve them. Decision-making and problem-solving are slightly different although interrelated processes. Planning provides a blueprint of what should be happening so that everyone knows what course has been charted and their respective roles and use of time in achieving the goals. Decision-making pervades planning activities. For example, a simple decision to increase production must be made within the context of its probable effects on employee use of time; the simple decision is actually complex and involves how much to raise production, when will the increase occur, which employees will be impacted, and a variety of other issues.

Decision-making is the process of choosing one alternative from among a set of alternatives. Problem-solving, on the other hand, occurs when someone is faced with an unfamiliar situation for which there are no established procedures that specify how to handle the problem. Dealing with eroding factors usually involves problem-solving. Often, information is received that indicates that something is wrong (e.g., turnover increases, more sick time is being used, employee complaints are up). Usually, only symptoms appear and some research, data gathering, or fact-finding must be done to uncover the true cause of the problem. It takes skill to separate symptoms from causes and properly diagnose the situation.

Rather than be seen as negative situations to be feared, problems should be seen as opportunities for making something new and creative happen. Whether problems are crises or opportunities, situations continuously arise in which people have little or no experience, no decision rules, and little or no guidance as to what to do. Managing time involves planning, decision-making, and, on occasion, problem-solving.

Determining your and your team's goals will involve planning. In particular, how you and your team need to plan how time will be used to contribute to the organization's value. In developing those plans, both decision-making and problem-solving will come into play.

Organizing is the process of grouping activities and resources in logical and appropriate ways in order to use time to contribute to the organization's value. In a sense, it is planning the work itself and is an enabling factor. Decisions that brought about the creation of a specific set of activities, as opposed to a different mix, are part of organizing. The determination of how many activities each person will have, the kinds of interactions among those people, and the activities themselves are all part of organizing as is how much time each activity is to have.

Controlling is the process of monitoring and adjusting the time required to carry out the organizational activities that are necessary to attain and maintain the organization's value in the marketplace. Monitoring progress and making appropriate adjustments is controlling. Consider the following example of the importance of time in the controlling function of management:

> Luke was late again. It seems like every time we need to meet; he is late. I don't know whether he just doesn't care, is just lazy, doesn't plan, or, maybe, he is trying to show how "powerful" he is and that schedules don't apply to him. I've taken to telling him that the meeting starts 15 minutes earlier than it really does to see if that will work.

Luke seems to not be able to control his time. He clearly needs to focus on his goals and develop plans. His manager has not created the culture that would help Luke have better use of his time.

Leading refers to you managing your time and guiding your subordinates or team members in the use of theirs. It is the set of processes associated with guiding and directing organizational members toward the best use of time in achieving the goals of the group. Key parts of leading are motivating people, managing group processes, and dealing with conflict and change. You must keep the group focused on the goals, help each member to handle stress, mediate conflicts, and, of course, you must manage your time and lead others to do the same.

All of these functions are involved as you manage your time. You plan how you will spend your time and assist others in planning their use of time. You organize your and others' activities so as to make the best use of everyone's time. You strive to control extraneous factors that would impede the best use of everyone's time. And, of course, you lead through example by properly managing your own use of time.

So, at this point, you must lead. You need to carefully analyze how you are using your time and use your analysis as an example for those in your group or team.

Management and Manager Questions

1. Do you have a "formal" managerial title? If not, do you nevertheless carry out one or more of the functions of a manager?
2. What eroding and enabling factors seem to exist in your organization?
3. How well do you understand your organization's value in the marketplace?

Management and Manager Actions

Discuss each of these concepts with your subordinates or team members to be sure everyone understands them.

5

Your Time

It's how we spend our time here and now, that really matters. If you are fed up with the way you have come to interact with time, change it.
—Marcia Wieder

At this point, you need to get a good understanding of just where you are now in terms of *quality time.* How productive are you? How are you handling time in your organization? To understand how you are currently handling time, you should complete the following assessment (You may find it easier to make a copy of the version in the Appendix rather than marking up the book). After completing your assessment, the analysis should suggest ways in which you as an individual could improve your use of time.

Quality Time, pages 29–33

Your Time Assessment (Also included in the Appendix)

Instructions

For each statement below, enter the number that indicates the degree to which you do each activity. Focus on achieving your organization's value and assess your behavior as it *is,* not as you would *like* it to be. How useful this instrument will depend on how accurately you assess your own behavior.

The first section of the instrument is general whereas the second section applies only to managers.

An analysis of the scores is provided at the end.

Rating Scale

6 Strongly agree	5 Agree	4 Slightly Agree	3 Slightly disagree	2 Disagree	1 Strongly disagree

Section I (General)

____ 1. I reach out to others for help in accomplishing my tasks.

____ 2. I set SMART goals (specific, measurable, achievable, realistic, time-specific).

____ 3. I strive to recognize how my tasks are related to the value of the organization.

____ 4. I prioritize according to importance and urgency.

____ 5. I skim read material until I find what is important and highlight it.

____ 6. I make a to-do list each day (tasks to accomplish).

____ 7. I make a list of short 5- or 10-minute tasks to do.

____ 8. I concentrate on only one important task at a time but do trivial tasks at once (like signing letters while talking on the phone).

____ 9. I do the most important tasks at my best time during the day.

____ 10. Where possible, I divide large projects into smaller, separate stages.

____ 11. I identify which 20% of my tasks will produce 80% of my results.

____ 12. I keep my work and personal items readily locatable.

____ 13. I have some time during each day when I can work uninterrupted.

____ 14. I don't procrastinate. I do it when it needs to be done.

____ 15. I keep track of my time (with tools such as a time log).

____ 16. I set deadlines for myself.

____ 17. I do something productive whenever I have to wait.

____ 18. I do redundant "busy work" at one time during the day.

____ 19. I finish at least one thing every day.

____ 20. I schedule a time during the day for personal time alone (for planning, meditation, prayer, exercise).

____ 21. I allow myself to worry about things only at one time of day, not all the time.

____ 22. I have clearly defined long-term objectives I am working toward.

____ 23. I continually try to find little ways to improve my efficient use of time.

____ 24. I say "no" to requests if they involve unwanted or unnecessary tasks.

____ 25. I block out distractions.

____ 26. I feel free to express my thoughts to managers and group members.

____ 27. I ask questions to clarify my assignments.

____ 28. I listen to others' points of view and remain open to changing my mind.

____ 29. I prepare for and actively participate in meetings of the group.

____ 30. I try to keep a time buffer between tasks and/or meetings.

Section II (Managers)

____ 1. I help others to see how their tasks are related to the value of the organization.

____ 2. I develop plans for each day and week.

____ 3. I know how to deal with interruptions.

____ 4. When team members or others come to me with a problem, I require that they first suggest solutions.

____ 5. I meet visitors to my office outside the office or in the doorway.

____ 6. I go to others' offices when feasible so that I control when I leave.

____ 7. I have someone else who can answer my calls and greet visitors at least some of the time.

____ 8. I have one place where I can work uninterrupted.

____ 9. I do something definite with every piece of paper I handle.

____ 10. I keep my workplace clear of all materials except those I am working on.

____ 11. I communicate widely so that others can readily assist in the accomplishment of goals.

____ 12. I delegate tasks to others.

____ 13. I specify the amount of personal initiative I want others to take when I assign them a task.

____ 14. I am willing that others get the credit for tasks they accomplish.

____ 15. I take breaks to keep myself fresh and alert.

____ 16. I leave at least one-fourth of my day free from meetings and appointments I can't control.

____ 17. I try to be open with others and sensitive to their moods and feelings.

____ 18. I mediate and resolve minor disputes by continually emphasizing the group's goals.

____ 19. I establish clear time frames for everyone so that everyone understands their responsibilities.

____ 20. I discuss with subordinates or team members the progress they are making.

With Respect to Meetings:

____ 21. I set time limits at the start of each meeting.

____ 22. I hold routine meetings at the end of the day.

____ 23. I hold all short meetings standing up.

____ 24. I cancel scheduled meetings that are not absolutely necessary.

____ 25. I have a written agenda for every meeting.

____ 26. I stick to the agenda and reach closure on each item.

____ 27. Someone is assigned to take minutes and to watch the time in every meeting.

____ 28. I start all meetings on time.

____ 29. I have minutes of meetings prepared promptly after the meeting and see that follow-up occurs promptly.

____ 30. I try to bring out divergent points of view.

_____ 31. I try to end each meeting with a clear plan of action.

_____ 32. I try to be flexible in terms of how we cover the agenda.

_____ 33. I ask that cell phones be turned off during meetings.

_____ 34. I follow-up with anyone who missed the meeting.

Your Time Assessment Results

Understanding how you currently are using your time is important and this assessment can help you adjust your use of time to more clearly focus on your role in achieving the organization's value. In addition, working through this assessment can help you to appreciate the issues your group or team faces. You should consider changing your behavior on items for which your scores were either 3 or 4. And you should definitely change your behavior on items for which your score was only 1 or 2.

But before making notes to yourself about changes, use your responses to think about eroding and enabling factors. What eroding factors can you identify based on this assessment? Can you envision ways in which those could be reduced if not eliminated? How about enabling factors? Have you identified any of those as well? What are they and how can you take full advantage of them? Are there some that could be enabling with some slight changes? To help you make changes suggested by the assessment and as you think about those factors, you need to carefully understand the impact of those on you and your subordinates or team members. With an eye toward managing your time better, consider how you would make the sort of changes raised in the next chapter.

Your Time Questions

1. Have you determined which of your goals are most important?
2. Do you have a "quiet hour" in which to carefully think through your and your team's activities?
3. Have you identified eroding and enabling factors?

Your Time Actions

Make a list of the behaviors for which you scored either 1 or 2 and then consider how you would change each of them. You might wish to do the same for those marked 3 or 4, too.

6

Adjusting Your Time

Yesterday is gone. Tomorrow has not yet come. We have only today. Let us begin.
—Mother Theresa

The enabling and eroding factors you just identified should guide adjustments to the use of your time and help you achieve *quality time.* Attempting to be so precise in your activities that you time things to seconds is an attempt to be efficient which is not necessarily effective. Rarely in every workday is such precision necessary. Indeed, building in some slack time may help to reduce stress and improve morale and productivity for both you and your team. Similarly, trying to see to it that others spend exact amounts of time on activities is also an attempt to be efficient which may not be effective. In each of these cases, your focus is on time instead of the organization's value and productivity goals so that short-term time savings are obtained at the cost of not achieving longer-term objectives. Your contribution to the value of the organization is reduced by such precise efforts. Focus on results, not the use of time to get the most from this assessment.

Quality Time, pages 35–43

Taking time from your personal life—self, family, friends, religion, community, and so on—to devote to your job so that you can accomplish more represents an effort to be effective, which is not efficient. You need time away from work to destress and reenergize. And having others in whom you can confide not only reduces stress but can also lead to different approaches to problems and creative solutions. Likewise, taking time from your superiors or team members to have them assist you in accomplishing your job is an effort to be effective, which is not necessarily efficient. In each of these cases, you add more of a scarce resource—time—to be more effective. You do not necessarily become efficient in doing so.

Accomplishing your objectives without having your life run by time clocks and without "borrowing" time from other people or from other activities is what you want to become good at doing. To do so means balancing efficiency and effectiveness. That balancing involves regulating your use of time in your activities.

Adjustments

Managing your time so as to contribute to your organization's value begins with understanding the process by which adjustment is achieved. Adjustment is the method by which you assure that your desired stress/time management ideas become reality. The basic process has several components—antecedents, actual behavior, desired behavior, results, and adjustments. That process can be visualized as in Figure 6.1.

In order to properly adjust your behavior, you need to have clear goals, prioritize them, and develop a plan. You must know both how you should be spending your time (desired behavior) and how you are spending your time now (actual behavior). You need to identify both eroding and enabling factors. After obtaining that information you will be in a position to consider what sort of adjustments would fit your particular situation. So, the first thing you must do is clearly identify your desired behavior. To determine what you should be doing with your time, you must first determine what you want to accomplish—what your goals are.

> Joe says he can't seem to get organized around his goals. He tends to react to whatever seems urgent at the time. His problem is that he hasn't tried to distinguish between long-term goals and short-term, day-to-day objectives. As a result, he spends too much time agonizing over whether he is really making progress on his goals or just "marking time."

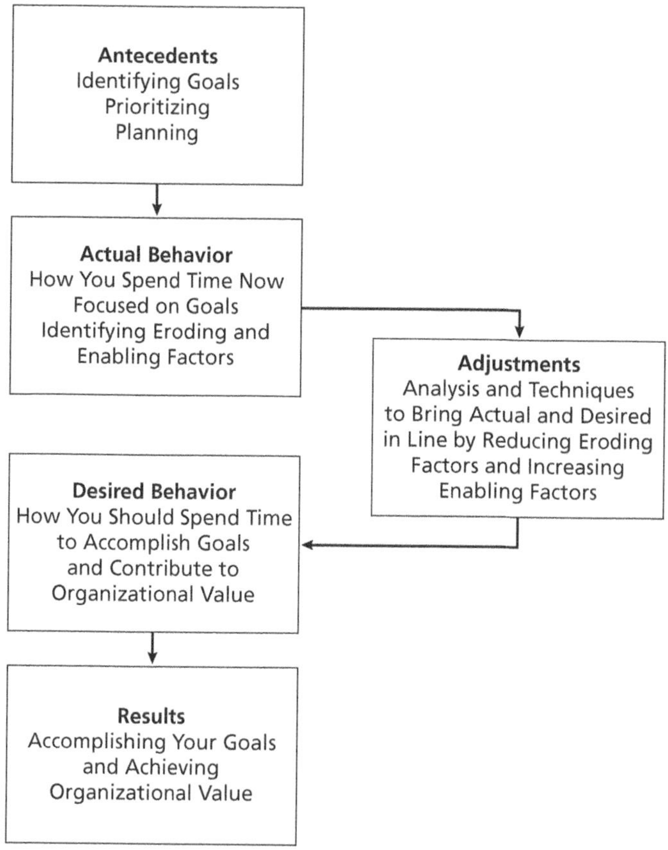

Figure 6.1 Adjustment process.

Personal Goals

What Joe needs to do is to clearly specify his goals by putting them in writing. The use of a personal goal sheet could be beneficial. Think about your goals in terms of "What do I need to do over the next few years to be on track to accomplish my longer-term ones?" Then use the same approach to determine what your short-term objectives should be to assure that you progress toward your intermediate goals. Start by being a bit selfish and think about what you personally would like to accomplish. Then move to family, jobs, and finally your community. As you develop your Personal Goal Sheet (Figure 6.2), you will see where things overlap or complement one another (enabling factors), and you will also see where real or potential

Goal Focus	Short-Term 3 months to 1 year	Transitional 3 to 5 years	Long-Term 7 to 10 years
Personal			
Family			
Job and Career			
Community and Profession			
Other			

Figure 6.2 Personal Goal Sheet (for determining how time should be spent). *Note:* The long-term goals should be broad, general ones. Seek the Appendix for a version to copy and use.

conflicts may arise (eroding factors). This will be the time to consider how to adjust your goals so as to avoid those conflicts.

The Personal Goal Sheet presented here (and in the Appendix) is just an example. While it is important to consider short to intermediate or transitional to long-term goals, the specific time frames could certainly vary with your position in the organization and the current stage of your career.

Likewise, the areas of goal focus could be simplified to just "self and job" or "self, family, and job" or expanded to include more possibilities and to cover more complex situations. You need to construct your personal goal sheet to fit your particular situation.

Once you have your goals identified, you need to prioritize them. Start with your long-term goals and develop priorities, which is most important, which is next, and so on. As you think about them, ask yourself if any are unrealistic and could be dropped. Then link the highest priority goals to intermediate-term goals and then back to short-term ones. This suggests how you should be spending your time—accomplishing your goals!

> Sara keeps a "to do" list and is very busy every day, but she seems to be missing the "big picture." She says that she just works through her list every day but if something doesn't get done, she just moves it to the top of the list for the next day. She gets things done but not necessarily things that are really important to someone in her position. She says that she is stuck in a rut and can't seem to make any progress toward what she really wants in her job and her life.

Means–End Analysis

Sara needs to recognize her priorities. One way she could do that would be to use a means-end staircase or chain means–end chain (Gutman, 1998; Lin, Jeng, & Yeh, 2018). This approach is known as *means–end analysis* or MEA and is frequently used by executives in strategic planning and marketing. However, you can use the basic approach to focus your use of time. To be successful, you need to think from large to small; the eventual goal needs to be split into smaller sub-goals. Focusing on your long-term goals can be overwhelming. So, you have to shift your thinking from goals to smaller objectives. Long-term goals are broken into smaller objectives. Those objectives are then boiled down into actionable steps or tasks to be performed.

Your personal goal sheet will suggest how your staircase should be developed. Figure 6.3 is an example of how your staircase might look for the highest priority goal. You would have similar ones for each high priority goal (usually only the top two or three). Breaking up a long-term goal into intermediate and then shorter-term objectives is a useful procedure to think about where you want to be and how you can get there. If you carefully build the staircase, then as long as you proceed from short to intermediate to long, your overall goals should be reached successfully. However, don't think of this as a static blueprint. Like all plans, it will need to be revisited over time as circumstances change. Some people revisit these annually while others suggest only every few years. Whatever review period

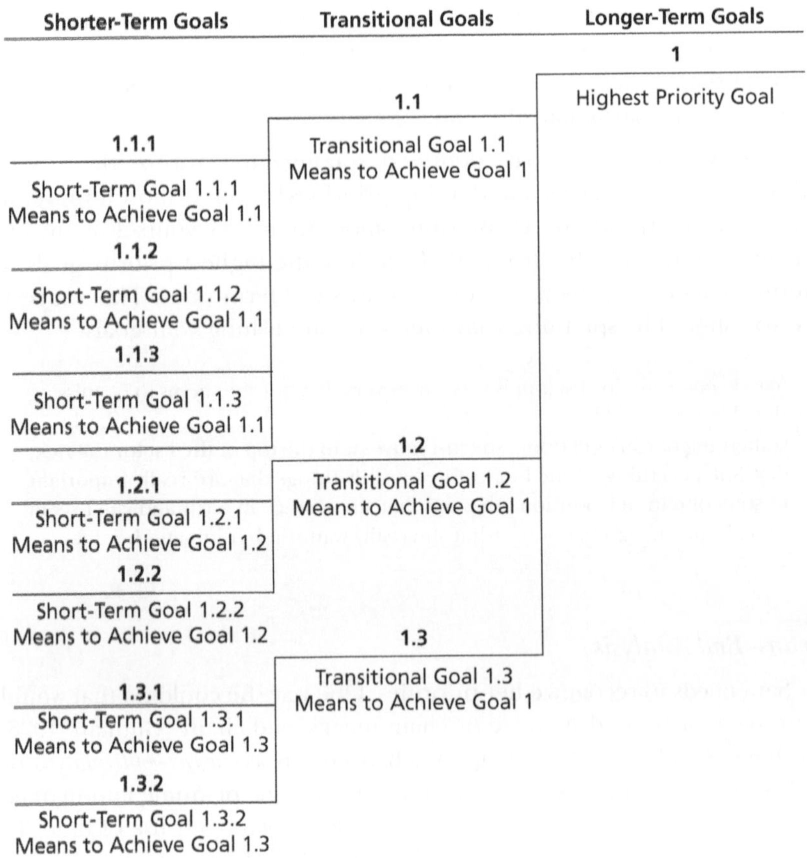

Figure 6.3 Means–end staircase.

you choose doesn't matter as much as taking the time to rethink the process periodically.

Again, this staircase shown here is only an example and it deals only with your number one or highest priority goal. Yours should have the three time frames for goals but the number of goals and the number of "steps" in the staircase will depend on your specific situation. Your longer-term goals should consist of only the top few highest priority ones. Don't spend time on goals that are of lesser importance.

Time Log

At this point, you have specified the antecedents for the regulatory process. Next, you must determine exactly how you actually are spending your time right now. You cannot simply rely on your memory for that—you must systematically find out by using some form of record keeping. While a manager's desk calendar is helpful, it does not provide the detail you really need. Some people keep a diary while others use a Daily Time Log (Figure 6.4).

The Daily Time Log shown here, however, is not likely to fit your particular circumstances—it is merely an example. Yours may start earlier or end later (or both). You may feel that 20-minute increments are too many (although much of your activity will almost certainly be in smaller chunks of time). Some users have larger increments but indicate that multiple activities occur within each block. You should develop yours in such a way that you can keep it up without undue disruption to your schedule. To be truly useful, you will need to complete not just one but several. Having several of them is suggested as no one day is exactly like every other. To be truly representative of the way you spend your time, plan on having several of these.

Time	Activity	Job	Non-Job	Comments
7:01–7:20				
7:21–7:40				
7:41–8:00				
8:01–8:20				
8:21–8:40				
8:41–9:00				
9:01–9:20				
9:21–9:40				
9:41–10:00				
↓				
3:41–4:00				
4:01–4:20				
4:21–4:40				
4:41–5:00				
5:01–5:20				
5:21–5:40				
5:41–6:00				
6:01–6:20				
6:21–6:40				
6:41–7:00				

Note: Where appropriate, record who initiated the activity (manager, team member, peer, family member, client, etc.

Figure 6.4 Daily time log (for recording how time is spent now). *Note:* See the Appendices for a complete version for copying and using.

You may even wish to space them out especially if certain days of the week are more demanding than others.

Summarization

After completing several daily time logs, summarize them to determine how you are actually spending your time now. Use a chart like the one shown in Figure 6.5 and be sure to note who initiated the activity (subordinate, supervisor, peer, or other). Try to do one for the first, last, and middle days of your workweek. An activity summary like the one shown here should help you with that task. Keeping track of the importance and urgency is important because you should be paying attention to those things that are important and not let something interfere just because it is urgent. Sometimes urgent tasks are best postponed if they don't contribute to goal achievement. But you should tailor the summary to fit your particular circumstances.

Finally, try to estimate the degree or extent to which each activity contributes to your personal goals—its importance in terms of goal attainment. However, you should have some quiet time, perhaps 30 minutes to an hour, without any interruptions for thinking about your job and your team. Remember you are trying to reach a situation where all of your activities contribute to the accomplishment of your goals.

At this point, you should have a good understanding of how you are using your time to help achieve the organization's value. So, now you need to shift your attention to your team.

Adjusting Your Time Questions

1. Did you use each of the "tools" shown here (personal goal sheet, means–end staircase, daily time log, activity summary)?
2. As you use these tools, are you able to identify eroding and enabling factors with respect to your time?

Adjusting Your Time Actions

Make a list of any changes you feel that you should make and set deadlines for making them. Focus particular attention on eroding and enabling factors in the V-REEL® framework. Try to develop specific steps to decrease eroding factors and increase enabling ones and move toward quality time.

Activity	Subordinate	Superior	Peer	Other	Importance	Urgency	Delegation
Desk Work							
Letters							
Memos							
Reports							
Periodocals							
Books							
Other							
Phone Calls							
Initiated							
Received							
Meetings							
Unscheduled							
Scheduled							
Travel							
Inside							
Outside							
Other							

Figure 6.5 Activity summary. *Note:* See the Appendix for a version intended for copying and using.

7

Managing Team Time

Rule number one is, don't sweat the small stuff. Rule number two is, it's all small stuff.

—Robert Eliot

Now that your individual goals and priorities have been established, it is time to focus on your group or team. You need to make copies of the assessment and the other "tools"—Personal Goal Sheet, Means-End Staircase, Daily Time Log, and Activity Summary—for each group or team member. Explain to them the meaning of *quality time*, the V-REEL® framework, and the importance of identifying both eroding and enabling factors. Then, demonstrate how to use the various tools and set a time for them to be completed, perhaps using yours as an example. It would be best if you could provide some time at work to encourage everyone to go through the exercise of completing all of these.

Once everyone has taken the assessment and established individual goals with priorities, it is time to focus specifically on the group or team itself.

Quality Time, pages 45–49

Using the new way of thinking about time in your organization, you and your group or team should employ the goal sheet and the means-end staircase for the team. They with your guidance should develop and prioritize the group goals and goals for the individual members of the group or team.

This requires communication among all parties. What is needed is a list of group or team goals along with priorities. Developing a means-end staircase for them is not an easy process as it may involve you, the manager, and individual group or team members having to rethink your and their individual sets of goals.

> Joe has complained that he feels left out on occasion. Others in the group don't always communicate with him about what's going on. He thinks he has some good ideas but doesn't seem able to get anyone to hear him out. His frustration is mounting and is causing him to pull away from the group. He has also begun to consider looking for another job.

You don't want to have any "Joes" in your group. Be sure that everyone's ideas and suggestions are heard and seriously considered.

The first step in managing group or team time is to assure that everyone understands the value of the organization and how their accomplishments contribute to that value. This would clearly help Joe and make the group more of a real team. Use the V-REEL framework to get this discussion going. While conceived for use in strategic management, it could be quite helpful in getting your group or team focused on productivity and performance. Have them discuss each of the V-REEL items and identify which eroding factors might be reduced and which enabling factors could be increased.

V = Value

How does the team see its contribution to the organization's value in the marketplace? What specific activities of the group or team are most important in this regard? A discussion surrounding these questions should enable your team to determine its longer-term goals.

R = Rareness

How rare is the group or team's potential in value creation? Are there other units in the organization that could also perform these activities? Can they develop unique characteristics that would make them stand out relative to other units in the organization?

E = Eroding Factors

What factors might reduce the group or team's ability to manage time and create value for the organization? Would unexpected changes (e.g., budget cuts) decrease their ability to accomplish their tasks? Is burnout due to stress by one or more members a possibility since that would clearly erode their ability to function at a high level? Are interdependencies with other organizational units restricting their ability to manage their time efficiently and effectively? Think about the examples already provided to stimulate a discussion of these factors.

E = Enabling Factors

What sort of support is needed for the group or team to continue to manage its time and create value? A better understanding of their means-end staircase should enable them to continue to be productive and perform well. Would changing schedules or adding a temporary employee help them to better accomplish their tasks? Would the application of technology in some form assist them in managing their time?

L = Longevity

How long will the situation continue before substantial changes may occur in the enabling or eroding factors? What can your group or team do to prepare for inevitable changes?

This is also a perfect time to activate the human capital of your group or team (Morrison, 2017). That approach involves adopting eight "principles."

1. Give people a purpose. Your group or team will develop its own purpose. Using the "tools" should accomplish this and result in a clear, understood, and accepted purpose for them. Your group or team members are more likely to internalize goals that they have helped set. Participation in goal setting is crucial.
2. Communicate widely. Involve everyone in this discussion. Don't censure any ideas or comments. Let everyone's thoughts and contributions be heard.
3. Accommodate change. Be ready to change if need be. Discussing the longevity factor will prepare the team for any upcoming changes.
4. Create a culture of worth. Show everyone their worth and show respect for everyone and their ideas. You should send a clear mes-

sage to all team members that they and their efforts are valued by the organization.

5. Create a culture of hope. As the manager, you need to smooth over any conflicts that may arise. By indicating your trust in the group or team and its members, you will also help the team develop confidence in its own performance.
6. Reward performance. While you should have clear connections between performance and organizational rewards, don't neglect the simple day-to-day rewards, especially intangible ones. Saying "good work" and "thanks" when appropriate can go a long way. Be sure to recognize the contributions of individual team members as well as that of the whole team.
7. Create a vision of participation in determining the future of the company. Use participation and delegation to support your team and its contribution to the value of the organization. This will enable you to build a strong culture necessary for long-term team and organization success.
8. Express gratitude. Be sure to say "thanks" to your group or team for their efforts. Let them know that you personally and the organization recognizes and values their contributions.

Having a group discussion about the V-REEL framework should be done once a year or any time that a major change in the team's assignment takes place. The first time will take longer than subsequent ones, so you need to allow for that in planning the activity. Perhaps an afternoon with the opportunity to socialize afterward would be sufficient. For groups or teams at higher levels in an organization, several days in a retreat or meeting away from the worksite might be required to establish compatible group and individual goals, priorities, and steps to be taken to assure the achievement of those goals. Groups or teams at lower organizational levels might need only a day or a few hours to accomplish this and again having the discussions offsite may improve open communications.

The next step, then, is for everyone to take action, to try to bring activities in line with goals to assure that the team is using its time to help the organization maintain its value. Numerous "tips" are discussed in the next chapter to assist you and your team to make any necessary adjustments.

Managing Team Time Questions

1. Have you determined which team goals are most important?

2. Have you examined how team members are spending time on those important goals?
3. Did you use each of the "tools" shown earlier (personal goal sheet, means-end staircase, daily time log, activity summary)?
4. What eroding and enabling factors have you identified?

Managing Team Time Actions

Make a list of any enabling and eroding factors identified in the team discussions and use time management tips and guidelines to support the enabling factors and to reduce the eroding ones.

8

Time Management Tips

Time is what we want most, but what we use worst.
—William Penn

In addition to the tools already discussed, here are some additional tips or suggestions to help you and your group or team be productive through adjustments to the use of time.

Kaizen

Kaizen is a Sino-Japanese word indicating "improvement," particularly, incremental improvement. While you should not expect tremendous impacts from your changes overnight, continuous small changes should give results rather quickly. It will take time to achieve *quality time* and some of your people will develop more slowly than others. Consider applying the 5 pillars or 5S associated with Kaizen (Gapp, Fisher, & Kobayashi, 2008; Hirano, 1995):

Quality Time, pages 51–55

1. *Seiri*—prioritize
2. *Seition*—organize so things can be found quickly
3. *Seiso*—keep the work area clean and uncluttered
4. *Seiketsu-Seiketsu*—have standard procedures to simplify the work
5. *Shitsuke*—self-discipline to show respect for others in your group or team

Philosophy

It is time quality, not time quantity, that counts. It is how you spend your time, not how much time you spend, that is truly important. Spending a lot of time on a project is not what matters; it is how you spend the time that is important. It is important that you take time to relax and do non-job activities, especially at night and on weekends. And remember the importance of interpersonal networks—don't cut off your friends.

Plan Goals

Keep your long-term goals in mind even when you are doing small tasks and unpleasant activities. Periodically review and revise your long-term goals and don't be surprised if they change. That is to be expected. You should also frequently review your short-term goals and be sure to identify daily activities that are necessary to accomplish them. Remember that effective planning saves future time and achieves better results even though it takes time to do it properly. Spending time now to save time in the future may well be worthwhile. Finally, concentrate on your objectives, not just staying busy. Don't confuse activity with results. Staying busy just to be busy is a sign of "workaholism" and prevents the achievement of quality time.

Prioritize

Prioritizing refers to recognizing an activity's importance in accomplishing longer-term goals. Remember that just because something is due "tomorrow" does not mean that it is a priority item. You need to avoid responding to urgent items if they are not priority ones. One way to make sure that you are properly focused is to use a daily "to-do" list—a list of specific items to be done each day.

> I tried to keep a list of things I should do each day but when I wrote them all down, I couldn't see how it would be possible to do them all. I was so de-

moralized that I just gave up trying to make a list. So, I just try to do whatever seems to be needed to be done at the time.

You need more than just a list. Be sure to arrange your "to do" items in priority order [A = highest priority = most likely to move you toward achieving your goals; B = intermediate priority; C = lowest priority]. Focus on accomplishing your "A's," not "B's" and certainly not "C's." Use a "C drawer" for storage of those items which you do not immediately throw away. Circumstances may change and an item in your "C drawer" may suddenly become a "B" or even an "A." Don't skip items on your "to-do" list just because they are difficult or unpleasant, especially "A" items.

The *Pareto* principle, which is commonly referred to as the 80/20 rule, suggests that approximately 80% of effects come from 20% of causes. In terms of time management, you should use it to remind you to keep focused on those things which are the highest priority [80% of your goal achievement will come from 20% of your activities—doing the "A" items]. Sometimes "A" items seem overwhelming. If so, try breaking them into a series of smaller items that can be more easily accomplished. This is known as the Swiss Cheese approach—poke enough holes and soon it is all gone. Do enough small parts to an overwhelming "A" and it, too, will soon be done.

Interruptions

When you are interrupted, consider the nature of the interruption and who is behind the interruption. An email marked as urgent may or may not really be urgent or important. A quick look is all that's necessary to decide whether to deal with it or save it for later. Whatever you do though, keep the interruption short. Don't allow it to sidetrack you from your activity.

Analyze

As you consider your goals and develop priorities, you should examine old habits for possible elimination or streamlining to reduce the time spent on them. As suggested earlier, keep a diary or time log to help you identify your major problems and opportunities. Look for times when you are most creative or productive and then try to schedule routine meetings and administrative duties at other times. Continually ask yourself, "What is the best use of my time right now?"

Employ Techniques

In addition to the use of "to do" lists, there are numerous other time management techniques that you should consider using. When you have to wait, consider that waiting time as a gift to relax, plan, or do something that you would otherwise not have done. Carry blank 3 × 5 cards or a small notebook to jot down ideas and notes while you wait. Use waiting time as a break. Even without waiting time, be sure to take breaks every now and then to rest; you will maintain your efficiency and productivity longer that way. And be sure to get a good night's sleep every day.

> Take a break! Get serious. I can't take a break. I've got way too much to do. Besides, if you take a break around here, people will think you're slacking, and your boss may find something else to assign to you. The only break I get is when I use the restroom but even then I feel the need to get back to work right away.

Maybe if you take an occasional break, you would find that you are more productive when you return to the task at hand.

With regard to "paper," generate as little paperwork as possible and throw away everything possible. Write replies directly on originals (keep a copy for yourself or keep the original and return the copy). Most importantly, do something with each piece of paper you handle—route to someone else, request other information before completion, and so on (this is sometimes referred to as "handling each piece of paper only once"). Concentrate on only one thing at a time. This also applies to electronic communication. Just because you got an email doesn't mean you have to respond and certainly doesn't mean you must respond immediately. Sometimes ignoring emails is the best strategy.

Dealing with others is especially challenging in terms of time management. Other people can help or hinder so there are some tips for dealing with them. Be considerate of others' time as you want them to be considerate of yours. This helps you establish a positive culture of worth. If your workplace permits, have visitors, mail, and phone calls screened (an answering machine can be used for phones). Have an "open door" policy that means that with Caller-ID you are accessible but not that you physically keep your door open. Start meetings on time (plus a minute or two) even if everyone is not present. Set deadlines for yourself and others. Delegate where feasible and practicable given time demands on others, and when you do delegate, be considerate of others' time.

Cell Phones

Cell phones, tablets, and laptop computers have become ubiquitous in today's workplaces and can be great time savers, but they can also be time wasters. You need to consider how you are using them, especially around others. When using your cell phone or voice recognition software speak softly to avoid disrupting others. Watch your language, especially when others can overhear you. Be courteous to those you are with; turn off your device if it will be interrupting a conversation or activity. If it must be on and it could bother others, use the "silent" mode and move away to talk. Pay attention during meetings; don't text.

Paradox

But as you consider how to employ these tips, you should also be aware of the paradox of time "No one has enough time, but everyone has all there is." (see the Appendices for more "paradoxes")

While using the "tools" and these tips should enable good progress for the team in its use of time to contribute to the organization's value, there will still be tension or stress in the day-to-day functioning of the team. So, consider how to handle that stress.

Time Management Tips Questions

1. Which tip or tips did you find most useful?
2. Do you use a "to do" list?
3. How much of a time interruption is your cell phone? The cell phones of others?
4. Do any of these tips help you to reduce eroding factors and/or increase enabling ones?

Time Management Tips Actions

Go over these tips with subordinates or team members and discuss openly any areas where potential conflict may occur; for example, where your "A" goal involves them, but they see their role as only a "B" or worse a "C." Focus on the V-REEL® framework and how it may help to identify "A" goals as you move toward quality time.

9

Time and Stress

It's not stress that kills us, it is our reaction to it.
—Hans Selye

It should be clear by now that seeking *quality time* to support the organization's value is stressful. So, just as time can be managed, so too can stress be managed. As indicated earlier, stress refers to an individual's reaction to a strong stimulus called a stressor. As noted in Chapter 2, the three-stage cycle (General Adaptation Syndrome [GAS]) can involve resistance to lessen the impact of stressors.

Understanding Stress

As shown in Figure 9.1, individuals can become more resilient so that the impact of stressors can be alleviated. A closer look will help clarify some approaches to developing resiliency.

Quality Time, pages 57–64

Figure 9.1 Stress.

Stressors

Time is the largest single stressor for managers in American organizations. While temporary time stressors (deadlines and overtime, for instance) can be enabling and increase motivation, a constant state of time pressure is harmful. Other stressors that are eroding factors include situational stressors at work (rapid change and poor working conditions) or in family or social life (new family member, family member illness, church or civic obligations, for example), encounter stressors (conflicts in roles, disagreements about contracts), and anticipatory stressors (expectations or fear that bad things are going to happen—loss of a job, contract, etc.).

> I'm always rushing. It seems like no matter what I've got planned for the day, something comes up and I have to rush to deal with it and then rush back to where I was only to then have to rush off for something else. I keep thinking "surely this could wait," but then I get panicky if I don't get right on it.

Time is a big stressor for many people but rushing from one task to another simply adds to the stress rather than relieving it.

Reactions

Research has found that time stress is related to a whole host of negative consequences. At the personal level, these include feeling anxious, irritable, or depressed, sleeping problems, fatigue, muscle tension or headaches, stomach problems, social withdrawal, loss of sex drive, and use of alcohol or drugs to cope. These also could show up at work as well as apathy, loss of interest in work, trouble concentrating, job dissatisfaction, tension, perceived threats, increased heart rate and/or cholesterol levels. And, of course, stress can impact your relations with those on your team.

Resiliency

Developing resiliency may not come easily. To become more resilient to the physical reactions to stress, you need to establish a physical program of conditioning and exercise. Take walks especially nature walks. Set aside time to relax and "get away from it all." Learn a relaxation technique such as meditation, yoga, or tai-chi to help relax and practice it regularly. To develop personal and social resilience, establish support persons and/or groups, do not withdraw or become hostile or depressed, but do develop time management, delegation, prioritizing, and planning skills. So, short-term, you strive to develop resiliency but long-term consider eliminating stressors by changing jobs, moving, or avoiding certain situations or individuals.

However, not all stress is bad. Without some level of stress, individuals become lethargic and don't do much of anything. An optimal level of stress, on the other hand, can result in motivation and excitement. So, the key is determining when stress is too little or too great. Typically, in organizations, stress levels tend to be high so reductions in stressors are generally in order, particularly if the stress is from time pressure.

As shown in Figure 9.2, the stress process can be seen as a bell-shaped curve. The left side represents positive or eustress which serves to enable

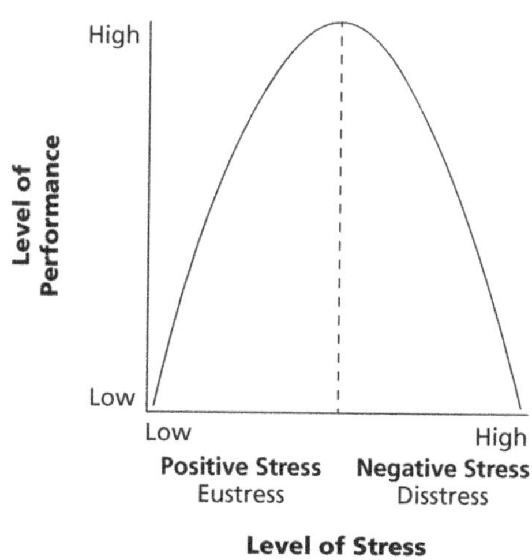

Figure 9.2 Stress and performance.

or motivate and hence increase performance. The right side is negative or distress that erodes and demotivates and decreases quality time and performance. Clearly, you want to use the concepts just discussed to decrease the eroding factors of your distress.

Stress Applications of Time Management

Consider these specific applications to control stress with time management. You are far less likely to experience unmanageable levels of stress while pursuing your own personal goals than when you feel "trapped" doing things that have no meaning to you. You can see how even boring, unpleasant tasks move you toward the achievement of goals in which you are interested. While you still must do things according to schedules, you are in control of your life, not someone else, not clocks nor calendars. Use waiting time for activities associated with your goals. That may be taking notes or developing ideas on your cell phone. It may be reading material that you need to read. Or it may be relaxing/resting so that you can be more productive after the wait is over.

And speaking of relaxing, stress is partially alleviated through rest and relaxation. This involves getting away from the pressure periodically—vacations, nights, weekends, and even by putting your feet up and closing your eyes for a few minutes every few hours while at work. Being in good physical condition enables you to handle more stress than you otherwise could. Exercise helps achieve that good physical condition. Finally, venting your frustrations and anger in constructive ways can ease your stress.

> Don keeps working on a project that should have been completed by now. He says that after he reviewed his work, it needed to be improved. He always seems unhappy with what he finally is forced to do because he says, "It could have been better." His perfectionism is hurting not just his performance but that of others who depend on him.

Don displays a problem seen in many high-performance organizations—attempting to be the "best," to "optimize," and to always seek perfection. There are ways of handling stress in such organizations.

Stress in High-Performance Organizations

High performance organizations continuously emphasize productivity and performance goals. There is little slack, and standards are high. Performance generally includes quality as well as quantity and extends to standards other than those which are most easily measured. Everything is focused tightly on accomplishing goals. High performance organizations raise expectations about performance continuously. They also generally require longer hours from their members although those hours may be spent at locations other than the work location itself, including home offices. As a result, stress levels can be quite high. These organizations tend to operate with a high level of group activity rather than relying exclusively on individual activity. This increases stress since cooperation and performance are important. But it also decreases stress by providing social support. If your organization is a high performance one, it is particularly important that you employ one or more of the time and stress management techniques.

Think about your situation. What are your major stressors? How do you try to cope with them? Do you exercise regularly? Does your organization provide facilities or services to help you manage stress? Does your organization or your particular unit attempt to use stress to motivate performance? Discuss with team members how each of you causes stress for the other and what might be done to alleviate that stress.

Before going further, you and your group members should get a good understanding of just where you are now in terms of handling stress in your organization. You and each of your group members should complete the following assessment. After completing your assessment, the analysis should suggest ways in which you could improve your use of time and move toward achieving quality time.

Stress Assessment

Instructions

Please respond to the following statements by writing a number from the rating scale by each item. Focus on achieving your organization's value so that your answers reflect your attitudes and behavior as they *are now*, not as you would *like* them to be. Be honest. This assessment is designed to help you discover your level of competency in handling stress so that you make improvements. An analysis is located at the end of this assessment.

The first section of the instrument is intended to be used by both you as a manager and everyone in your group. The second section applies only to you as a manager.

Rating Scale

6 Strongly agree	5 Agree	4 Slightly Agree	3 Slightly disagree	2 Disagree	1 Strongly disagree

Section I (General)

When faced with a stressful situation:

____ 1. I try to focus on how I contribute to the value of the organization.

____ 2. I take deep breaths or use meditation, yoga, or tai-chi to help me relax.

____ 3. I count to 10 before I speak or react to something someone did or said.

____ 4. I regularly exercise.

____ 5. I try to eat healthy, well-balanced meals.

____ 6. I make sure to get a good night's sleep of about 8 hours.

____ 7. I use time-management methods to reduce time pressure.

____ 8. I concentrate only on high priority tasks.

____ 9. I don't let work drive away my life outside the organization.

____ 10. I go outdoors for walks to cool down.

____ 11. I have a close friend with whom I can share my frustrations.

____ 12. I seek help from others to get my work done.

____ 13. I encourage others to make suggestions about getting work done.

____ 14. I always thank others for their support and contributions.

____ 15. I try to think of problems as opportunities for improvement.

____ 16. I monitor my use of caffeine, nicotine, and sugar intake.

____ 17. I listen to soft music to help me calm down.

____ 18. If a stressful task is not urgent, I sleep on it and get to it tomorrow.

____ 19. I have a hobby to help me relieve stress.

____ 20. I keep a stress journal to better understand and deal with things or people that cause me stress.

Section II (Manager)

To reduce my stress, I may delegate tasks to others. When I do:

____ 21. I make sure they see how the task is related to the value of the organization.

____ 22. I select the individual based on his or her ability and training needs.

____ 23. I try to assign a whole task rather than merely parts.

____ 24. I provide the necessary resources and authority to accomplish the tasks.

____ 25. I keep them informed as new information and resources come available.

____ 26. I specify the level of performance expected.

____ 27. I have the person agree on a schedule and deadline.

____ 28. I make sure that the person understands exactly what I want them to do.

____ 29. I follow up and maintain accountability for delegated tasks.

____ 30. I always thank them when they are finished.

____ 31. I identify the reason for the task and how it contributes to the group goals as well as to the individual.

____ 32. I reward successful task completion.

____ 33. I don't constantly keep checking on progress.

____ 34. I invite feedback on how and to whom I delegate.

____ 35. I make sure the person is willing and able to accept the task.

Stress Assessment Analysis

This assessment is designed to help you discover your level of competency in handling stress so that you make improvements. The higher your scores, the better you are at dealing with stress.

You should encourage those in your group to consider changing their behavior on items for which their scores were either 3 or 4. You should strongly encourage them to change their behavior on items for which their score was only 1 or 2. Likewise, you should consider changing your behavior on items for which your scores are either 3 or 4, and you should definitely change your behavior on items for which your score was only 1 or 2.

To help you make those and other changes, consider the guidelines in the next chapter.

Stress Management Questions

1. What are your major stressors?
2. Does your organization or your particular unit attempt to use stress to motivate performance?
3. What sort of resiliency techniques are you using?
4. Are your stressors eroding factors or enabling factors?

Stress Management Actions

Discuss with subordinates or team members how each of you causes stress for the other and what might be done to alleviate that stress. Focus on how stress can erode your team's management of time but also on how it can enable more efficient and effective time management.

10

Help Is on the Way

You cannot do a kindness too soon, for you never know how soon it will be too late.
—Ralph Waldo Emerson

Now consider some guidelines that should help you in both dealing with stress and in achieving *quality time.*

Handling Work

Be sure that your productivity goals contribute to the creation and maintenance of your organization's value in the marketplace (adapted from Flint, 2018; Morrison, 2017). Help your subordinates or team members learn the tools and techniques of time management. Combine tasks to gain efficiency, such as forming identifiable work units—groups or teams working on similar or related tasks. To assure effectiveness, be certain that everyone knows the overarching goal of the organization and their individual goals associated with it.

Quality Time, pages 65–70

Communicate widely by opening channels of communication with clients/customers as well as subordinates or team members. Focus your communications on goals and performance and avoid personal criticisms as they could erode your influence with others. Remember that not everyone has the same background, so what is clear to one person may not be clear to another. In particular, be careful when using technical terms; translate them when necessary. Try to illustrate what you mean and allow for questions to assure that you are being understood.

Beware of time-wasting communication and meetings as they could erode quality time and your contribution to your goal achievement. Develop enabling factors by creating a culture that builds on the value of individuals and provides them with hope.

> My boss and my subordinates drive me crazy. I'm always having to wait for them to do something or make up their minds. I waste so much time waiting around for them that it's a miracle that I get anything done. Half the time I think that I'll just go ahead and take a stab at the task but I'm afraid that if I do, I'll just have to redo it once I hear from them.

As noted earlier, use waiting time to advantage rather than permitting it to increase your stress.

If the purpose of the communication is to provide feedback, you need to be especially careful. You should focus on how performance contributed to or detracted from the accomplishment of the group or team goals. Try to describe what was good or poor in terms of behavior and performance and avoid personality issues. Make the feedback forward-looking—what can be done in the future rather than what was done in the past. And, of course, ask questions to assure that the message was received.

Use proversity or progressive diversity (Graham, 1997). Diverse workplaces can be stressful but can also be significant sources of creativity and innovation. Proversity involves first recognizing and eliminating your own biases, expanding your universe of contacts, showing respect for all individuals, and openly discussing differences. This will go a long way toward creating a culture of worth and hope. Assure that your role in the organization's culture truly encompasses the set of values that helps organization members understand what the organization stands for, how it does things, and what it considers important. Building that culture will involve recognizing the value of people in your organization by treating them fairly, rewarding performance, and encouraging participation. Show confidence in others by delegating tasks to them.

Show respect for others. "R E S P E C T—all I'm asking is a little respect" (Otis Redding's "Respect" song [Stax Records, 1965], made popular by Aretha Franklin) sets the framework. People want respect from others and particularly from supervisors. Understanding the perspective of others in the organization is critical, as is working around individual differences as members of an organization develop understanding and respect for one another. It is important to exercise care so that preferential treatment does not occur and is not perceived as occurring.

Showing respect while delegating means knowing your people so well that you avoid under- or over-delegating. Under-delegation occurs when you give someone such a trivial task that it is almost insulting. It shows that you have little confidence in them—that you don't trust them. Insecure managers are prone to do this as are micromanagers, who feel that they must be in control of everything all the time. Over-delegation occurs when you give someone a task that is beyond their capabilities. You overestimated what they could do or perhaps you failed to provide the necessary resources or were too vague in what was expected.

Closely associated with over-delegation is inundation, which is an eroding factor and decreases quality time. Inundation occurs when you overload someone probably because they are good at a variety of tasks, so you just keep assigning them tasks until they suffer a breakdown or just quit. And be careful to avoid reverse delegation, where a member of your group brings an assignment back to you, so you end up doing it anyway.

What you should do initially is sort tasks into four categories: delete, defer, delegate, do. Delete tasks are likely to be the C's referred to earlier. If you can't readily delete the task, put it off to a time when you can handle it better or consider delegating it to someone else. Otherwise, do it yourself and get it off your plate. Tasks such as returning phone calls and responding to emails should be deferred and handled in blocks of time instead of one at a time. As you sort tasks, think positive. Instead of thinking it can't be done, think about how it might be done. Instead of feeling helpless, reach out to others. Instead of thinking that you screwed up, think about mistakes as a learning experience.

Develop Your Team

Whatever your unit or group is actually called, you can accomplish more if it truly functions as a team. There are steps that you can take to help your group become a team. The primary step is for you to make a commitment to your group that you are there to support them, to help them achieve their personal goals while at the same time achieving organizational ones. You should encourage them to cooperate and think about the others in the team—what are their abilities and strengths that can contribute to the organization's value.

Make more of your communications based on "we" and "us" rather than "me" or "you." Get everyone thinking as a team rather than as individuals. As the team begins to work together, encourage them to share information and communicate widely. You should be open to suggestions from them and listen to any concerns that they may have. Ask them how they are doing and what you can do to assist them. Set clear expectations for performance and involve your team in establishing how performance will be measured. Above all, be open and honest in all of your dealings with your team.

Delegate

While delegation has already been discussed, you should recognize that many managers resist delegation. Hopefully, that does not include you; but some managers want more assignments and so don't delegate. Other managers have not assured that their subordinates are competent. Still others fear that they will lose recognition and rewards because their subordinates are actually doing the tasks. Finally, some managers simply prefer to do nonmanagerial work and so fail to delegate.

On the other hand, you should not delegate just to delegate. You should delegate only when it will increase performance, and delegate only those things that can be done as well as or better by the other person. You may also wish to delegate things so that your team members develop and grow on the job. Start with the routine, time-consuming jobs that you know someone else can do. Recognize that teaching someone else how to do a task will take some time. So, allow for a reasonable learning curve, but remember that it will pay off later.

> I can honestly say that I see at least two sides to every argument and pros and cons to every decision. But I can't seem to decide which side is stronger or whether the pros outweigh the cons. So, I end up delaying and then having to just mentally "flip a coin." And then I think I may have made the wrong decision.

Delegation, participation, and open discussions should alleviate such ambiguity and enable everyone to perform better.

When you do delegate, make sure that any mistakes are turned into learning experiences for the team member. Be sure to provide access to information and other resources that your team member will need to successfully accomplish the task. When they raise questions about the assignment, insist that they first suggest solutions to problems before you help them. You should provide support and assistance but avoid reverse delegation—where they simply put the monkey back on your back.

Also, when you do delegate, do so completely and clearly. Make certain that team members understand exactly what they are to do and that they have the authority to do so. Encourage participation and active communication in the process. Finally, make certain to hold team members accountable for the delegation and make certain that they understand that they will be held accountable through clear reporting mechanisms and timetables.

Handle Meetings

As a manager, you will hold numerous meetings. Many things can go wrong with meetings. A meeting may be held with no real purpose or agenda. Even with an agenda, discussions can go off the track. The meeting may start late or go too long to be productive. The wrong people may be at the meeting so it may be irrelevant to some. A few people may dominate discussion so there is little real participation among the attendees. People may come to the meeting unprepared or with hidden agendas. The meeting may end without having accomplished anything. And there may be no follow-up to the meeting, leading participants wondering what happened.

Some meetings will consist of just you and one other person while other meetings will be with a larger group. Those meetings may be informal or formal, planned or spontaneous, but all need to be controlled. You should hold short meetings (usually informal ones) standing up. Hold creative meetings early in the day and routine meetings at the end of the day. Put time limits on all meetings. For more formal meetings, schedule them regularly and cancel them when due to changing circumstances they are no longer needed. Be sure to start on time and have an agenda. Have someone take minutes (rotate this among participants) and distribute the minutes promptly after the meeting and to follow up with any issues not completely resolved during the meeting.

You want your meetings to be successful and the primary way to assure that is by engaging everyone in a positive discussion. Go around the room and ask each person for his or her ideas or opinions. Don't criticize anyone's ideas but rather be supportive and ask for clarification or elaboration.

When differences occur, try to mediate them and seek common ground about which everyone can get on board. Develop an action plan—what should be done based on this meeting.

If the meeting is to deal with a problem, five "steps" are needed—identify the problem, analyze or diagnose the problem, generate solutions, evaluate them, and finally choose one. When identifying the problem, make its presentation brief and to the point. Share all necessary information being careful to avoid suggesting causes or solutions and call upon the mutual interests of others in the group. As the problem is analyzed or diagnosed, alternatives should be considered and evaluated. Each alternative may suggest one or more solutions, so you need to assure that the group focuses on the present and considers novel or out of the ordinary solutions. As the group evaluates the solutions, advantages and disadvantages, costs and benefits need to be identified as well as the time necessary to do them right. Finally, of course, a solution must be chosen. In some situations, you as a manager must make that decision while in other cases, the group makes the decision.

The guidelines presented here should not only help you in identifying eroding and enabling factors but also suggest ways of reducing the erosion and strengthening the enabling factors.

Help Is on the Way Questions

1. Do you use participation?
2. Do you delegate?
3. Do you use proversity?
4. How do you handle meetings?
5. What eroding and enabling factors were identified in this chapter?

Help Is on the Way Actions

Discuss with your team members participation and delegation and how those concepts would help in achieving quality time. Identify eroding and enabling factors. Do the same for how meetings are handled. Are meetings eroding or enabling? Why?

11

What's Next

You will never find time for anything. If you want time you must make it.
—Charles Buxton

Summarizing what has been shown to achieve *quality time.*

- You first established the value you and your group or team contribute to the organization.
- You developed an appreciation for eroding and enabling factors impacting your use of time.
- You used an assessment to help determine just what those factors are in your situation.
- You then involved your group or team so that everyone would be "on the same page."
- Finally, a stress assessment was conducted to help you manage the stress that this process entails.

Quality Time, pages 71–76

Hopefully, you now have a better understanding of how you as an individual or as a manager can accomplish quality time in your organization. To gain the most from the ideas presented here, you should repeat the assessments in a few months to see what progress you have made as an individual. That should provide sufficient time to break old habits and establish new and better ways of managing time. Be sure to have your team members do the same. Having open discussions about time with your team is a major step toward establishing effective use of time to help create and maintain value for the organization. "Keep your eyes on the prize" (Seeger, 2020). *Remember that it's not the time that counts but how you use the time.*

But if you've gotten this far, perhaps you should consider other approaches to time at work that are being tried by various organizations. The timing of work hours and the degree to which individuals are able to exercise control over it are important enabling factors of workers' motivation, behavior, and effort at work. While you and your group may not be authorized to implement these, being aware of the possibilities would prepare you for possible changes should they come.

The New Norm

As this book goes to press, the world is trying to ride out the Coronavirus pandemic, which is forcing changes that affect not only their organizations but also their suppliers and consumers. The resulting enormous and unexpected challenges have required organizations to develop alternative work/time arrangements. These new challenges will cause management and workers alike to consider adopting some of the new ways as "the new norm" in the post Covid-19 era. These new norms will activate human capital that requires organizations to ensure equity, consistency, and a long-term orientation (Powell & Mainiero, 2010; Golden, 2003).

No doubt the world of work will never go back to exactly what it had been for countless millions of workers and teams. These changes make a reconsideration of how to manage groups and teams more important than ever. We can expect that many employees in many industries, particularly those associated with food, will wear gloves and masks. Restaurants may have disposable menus. Greeting and saying goodbye with a handshake, hug, or other forms of touching may become less common. Air travel may be limited to fewer flights and fewer seats with more restrictions in terms of security. Workstations will likely be farther apart, and more work will be done remotely—"at home" and online. Workdays and weekend days may become blurred. Regardless of how your organization responds to the new norm, it will need to be flexible and ready to adapt to changing conditions.

Some organizations already have attempted to be more flexible and adapt to changing conditions by resorting to the use of contingent work. Contingent work involves using employees only when needed. This would include part-time work, temporary help, employee leasing, self-employment, contracting out, and home-based work (Polivka, 1996). While contingent work is potentially beneficial to organizations, the use of contingent workers is rarely in the interests of employees except perhaps for students, parents of young children, and employees nearing retirement. So contingent work is unlikely either to activate the human capital of the organization or achieve quality time.

Numerous approaches that have been effective in some settings for both employees and organizations have been tried. Only when they increase employees' control over when and where they work will these approaches be successful (Gerstel & Clawson, 2018; Kelly & Moen, 2007). The most frequently used approaches are compressed or condensed workweeks, customized working hours, flexible vacation time, flextime, job-sharing, remote working, and telecommuting. Briefly, here are the basics characteristics for each of these.

Compressed or Condensed Workweeks

The most common compressed workweek is the four 10-hour day schedule. Less commonly used is the 9/80 schedule, in which employees work 80 hours in nine days and have one additional day off every other week. A typical schedule for the first week would be 9 hours Monday through Thursday with 4 hours on Friday morning. The second week begins with 4 hours that Friday afternoon followed by 9 hours Monday through Thursday with that following Friday off. Both of these require long hours but provide more days off and so appeal to some employees but not all.

Customized Working Hours

This approach allows employees to choose their own work hours (within reason). This allows individuals to fit their work schedules with their own biorhythm and personal or family expectations. The most common version of this approach is to let employees choose their hours in a window (such as starting anywhere from 6:00 a.m.–9:00 a.m.).

Flexible Vacation Time

Sometimes the phrase "unlimited paid time off" is used, but generally, the idea is to provide (with sufficient notification) employees the freedom to plan the vacation schedule that works best for them. Small organizations and start-ups seem to have originated this approach, but large corporations such as General Electric, Honeywell, Kronos, and Netflix offer similar benefits ("14 Cool Companies," 2018).

Flextime

Flextime is similar to customized work hours in that it provides employees greater latitude in choosing their particular hours of work, or freedom to change work schedules from one week to the next depending on the employee's personal needs. Typically, this approach requires employees to work a standard number of core hours within a specified period but allows them greater flexibility in their starting and ending times.

Job Sharing

This is not a very common approach, but it can be the right fit for some situations. Job sharing is similar to part-time work. It involves having two different employees performing the tasks of one full-time position. Each employee is part-time but together they account for the tasks of one full-time position. It requires a high degree of compatibility, communication, and cooperation between the job-sharing partners and with their supervisor.

Remote Working

Remote work is performed entirely away from the physical location of the organization. This approach may involve a permanent position or be only temporary (such as an employee traveling on business). It is generally used by organizations to broaden their applicant pool and for job descriptions that don't require in-person work. To be successful, however, careful goals and objectives must be established and frequent communication including video conferencing may be required. Remote working has been especially popular during the Covid-19 pandemic because it separates employees.

Telecommuting

Telecommuting is similar to remote working but consists of working remotely only part of the time. Employees come to the physical location 2 or 3 days a week and are on call for other times when needed. It usually involves full-time positions and can be implemented with nearly any position that doesn't require the worker to be in-office all the time.

These are the most common approaches, but organizations continue to experiment to find what works best for them. One of the most recent and unusual approaches is the 5-hour workday.

5-Hour Workday

Rheingans Digital Enabler, a Bielefeld-based consulting firm in Germany is experimenting with this approach. The 16 employees must put their cellphones away and keep small talk to a minimum. Further, they are permitted to check company emails only twice a day, and meetings are typically 15 minutes or shorter. Salaries, benefits, paid vacation time all remained at the same levels. Employees admit it required getting accustomed to not texting family members and to producing the same amount of work in 3 fewer hours daily. But reportedly they are happier and are spending more time with their families, exercising, tackling chores, and pursuing hobbies. The firm also reports that it is easier to recruit employees in Germany's tight labor market. The San Diego company Tower Paddle Boards also began a 5-hour workday in 2015, but 2 years later limited that schedule to just 5 months of the year after the CEO noted that their "passion for work" declined (Tedder, 2019).

All of these approaches strive to help both employees and the organization. However, none work unless the human capital of the organization is activated. As noted earlier, that means creating a culture in which employees are full participants in the approach. There must be a clear purpose where everyone's ideas are valued and in which people are thanked and rewarded for the contributions to the organization's value.

There are several benefits that may accrue to your organization if it is successful in a new work arrangement. Productivity will tend to increase and along with that costs are likely to be reduced. Your organization should be able to obtain favorable public relations by gaining a reputation as a good corporate citizen that is committed to employee well-being. This then provides a competitive advantage in the labor market as high-quality individuals will seek out your organization. And as your organization takes advantage of those individuals, productivity will increase and costs decrease even more.

Your and your group's understanding of the organization's value as well as eroding and enabling factors will assist everyone to achieve quality time and successful performance. After all, as has been emphasized before, *it is not the time but the performance that matters.*

Appendices

Assessments and "Tools" for Copying for Others

Make copies of each assessment and tool for each group or team member. After they are completed, use the results in discussing enabling and eroding factors.

Quality Time, pages 77–90

Personal Time Assessment

Instructions

For each statement below, enter the number that indicates the degree to which you do each activity. Assess your behavior as it *is,* not as you would *like* it to be. The usefulness of this instrument will depend on how accurately you assess your own behavior.

The first section of the instrument is general whereas the second section applies only to managers.

An analysis of the scores is provided at the end.

Rating Scale

6 Strongly agree	5 Agree	4 Slightly Agree	3 Slightly disagree	2 Disagree	1 Strongly disagree

Section I (General)

____ 1. I reach out to others for help in accomplishing my tasks.

____ 2. I set SMART goals (specific, measurable, achievable, realistic, time-specific).

____ 3. I strive to recognize how my tasks are related to the value of the organization.

____ 4. I prioritize according to importance and urgency.

____ 5. I skim read material until I find what is important and highlight it.

____ 6. I make a to-do list each day (tasks to accomplish).

____ 7. I make a list of short 5- or 10-minute tasks to do.

____ 8. I concentrate on only one important task at a time but do trivial tasks at once (like signing letters while talking on the phone).

____ 9. I do the most important tasks at my best time during the day.

____ 10. Where possible, I divide large projects into smaller, separate stages.

____ 11. I identify which 20% of my tasks will produce 80% of my results.

____ 12. I keep my work and personal items readily locatable.

____ 13. I have some time during each day when I can work uninterrupted.

____ 14. I don't procrastinate. I do it when it needs to be done.

____ 15. I keep track of my time (with tools such as a time log).

____ 16. I set deadlines for myself.

____ 17. I do something productive whenever I have to wait.

____ 18. I do redundant "busy work" at one time during the day.

____ 19. I finish at least one thing every day.

____ 20. I schedule a time during the day for personal time alone (for planning, meditation, prayer, exercise).

____ 21. I allow myself to worry about things only at one time of day, not all the time.

____ 22. I have clearly defined long-term objectives I am working toward.

____ 23. I continually try to find little ways to improve my efficient use of time.

____ 24. I say "no" to requests if they involve unwanted or unnecessary tasks.

____ 25. I block out distractions.

____ 26. I feel free to express my thoughts to managers and group members.

____ 27. I ask questions to clarify my assignments.

____ 28. I listen to other's points of view and remain open to changing my mind.

____ 29. I prepare for and actively participate in meetings of the group.

____ 30. I try to keep a time buffer between tasks and/or meetings.

Section II (Managers)

____ 1. I help others to see how their tasks are related to the value of the organization.

____ 2. I develop plans for each day and week.

____ 3. I know how to deal with interruptions.

____ 4. When team members or others come to me with a problem, I require that they first suggest solutions.

____ 5. I meet visitors to my office outside the office or in the doorway.

____ 6. I go to others' offices when feasible so that I control when I leave.

____ 7. I have someone else who can answer my calls and greet visitors at least some of the time.

____ 8. I have one place where I can work uninterrupted.

____ 9. I do something definite with every piece of paper I handle.

____ 10. I keep my workplace clear of all materials except those I am working on.

____ 11. I communicate widely so that others can readily assist in the accomplishment of goals.

____ 12. I delegate tasks to others.

____ 13. I specify the amount of personal initiative I want others to take when I assign them a task.

____ 14. I am willing that others get the credit for tasks they accomplish.

____ 15. I take breaks to keep myself fresh and alert.

____ 16. I leave at least one-fourth of my day free from meetings and appointments I can't control.

____ 17. I try to be open with others and sensitive to their moods and feelings.

____ 18. I mediate and resolve minor disputes by continually emphasizing the group's goals.

____ 19. I establish clear time frames for everyone so that everyone understands their responsibilities.

____ 20. I discuss with subordinates or team members the progress they are making.

With Respect to Meetings:

____ 21. I set time limits at the start of each meeting.

____ 22. I hold routine meetings at the end of the day.

____ 23. I hold all short meetings standing up.

____ 24. I cancel scheduled meetings that are not absolutely necessary.

____ 25. I have a written agenda for every meeting.

____ 26. I stick to the agenda and reach closure on each item.

____ 27. Someone is assigned to take minutes and to watch the time in every meeting.

____ 28. I start all meetings on time.

____ 29. I have minutes of meetings prepared promptly after the meeting and see that follow-up occurs promptly.

____ 30. I try to bring out divergent points of view.

_____ 31. I try to end each meeting with a clear plan of action.

_____ 32. I try to be flexible in terms of how we cover the agenda.

_____ 33. I ask that cell phones be turned off during meetings.

_____ 34. I follow-up with anyone who missed the meeting.

Your Time Assessment Results

Understanding how you are using your time is important and this assessment can help you adjust your use of time to more clearly focus on your role in achieving the organization's value. In addition, working through this assessment can help you to appreciate the issues your group or team faces. You should consider changing your behavior on items for which your scores were either 3 or 4. And you should definitely change your behavior on items for which your score was only 1 or 2.

Use your responses to think about eroding and enabling factors. What eroding factors can you identify? Can you envision ways in which those could be reduced if not eliminated? How about enabling factors? What are they and how can you take full advantage of them? To make changes suggested by the assessment and as you think about those factors, you need to understand the impact of those on you and your team members.

Personal Goal Sheet
(for determining how time should be spent)

Goal Focus	Short-Term 3 months to 1 year	Transitional 3 to 5 years	Long-Term 7 to 10 years
Personal			
Family			
Job and Career			
Community and Profession			
Other			

Note: The long-term goals should be broad, general ones.

Daily Time Log
(for recording how time is spent now)

Time	Activity	Job	Non-Job	Comments
7:01–7:20				
7:21–7:40				
7:41–8:00				
8:01–8:20				
8:21–8:40				
8:41–9:00				
9:01–9:20				
9:21–9:40				
9:41–10:00				
10:01–10:20				
10:21–10:40				
10:41–11:00				
11:01–11:20				
11:21–11:40				
11:41–12:00				
12:01–12:20				
12:21–12:40				
12:41–1:00				
1:01–1:20				
1:21–1:40				
1:41–1:00				
2:01–2:20				
2:21–2:40				
2:41–2:00				
3:01–3:20				
3:21–3:40				
3:41–4:00				
4:01–4:20				
4:21–4:40				
4:41–5:00				
5:01–5:20				
5:21–5:40				
5:41–6:00				
6:01–6:20				
6:21–6:40				
6:41–7:00				
Note: Where appropriate, record who initiated the activity (manager, team member, peer, family member, client, etc.				

Activity Summary

Activity	**Subordinate**	**Superior**	**Peer**	**Other**	**Importance**	**Urgency**	**Delegation**
Desk Work							
Letters							
Memos							
Reports							
Periodocals							
Books							
Other							
Phone Calls							
Initiated							
Received							
Meetings							
Unscheduled							
Scheduled							
Travel							
Inside							
Outside							
Other							

Stress Assessment

Instructions

Please respond to the following statements by writing a number from the rating scale by each item. Focus on achieving your organization's value so that your answers reflect your attitudes and behavior as they *are now*, not as you would *like* them to be. Be honest. This assessment is designed to help you discover your level of competency in handling stress so that you make improvements. An analysis is located at the end of this assessment.

The first section of the instrument is intended to be used by both you as a manager and everyone in your group. The second section applies only to you as a manager.

Rating Scale

6 Strongly agree	5 Agree	4 Slightly Agree	3 Slightly disagree	2 Disagree	1 Strongly disagree

Section I (General)

When faced with a stressful situation:

_____ 1. I try to focus on how I contribute to the value of the organization.

_____ 2. I take deep breaths or use meditation, yoga, or tai-chi to help me relax.

_____ 3. I count to 10 before I speak or react to something someone did or said.

_____ 4. I regularly exercise.

_____ 5. I try to eat healthy, well-balanced meals.

_____ 6. I make sure to get a good night's sleep of about 8 hours.

_____ 7. I use time-management methods to reduce time pressure.

_____ 8. I concentrate only on high priority tasks.

_____ 9. I don't let work drive away my life outside the organization.

_____ 10. I go outdoors for walks to cool down.

_____ 11. I have a close friend with whom I can share my frustrations.

_____ 12. I seek help from others to get my work done.

_____ 13. I encourage others to make suggestions about getting work done.

____ 14. I always thank others for their support and contributions.

____ 15. I try to think of problems as opportunities for improvement.

____ 16. I monitor my use of caffeine, nicotine, and sugar intake.

____ 17. I listen to soft music to help me calm down.

____ 18. If a stressful task is not urgent, I sleep on it and get to it tomorrow.

____ 19. I have a hobby to help me relieve stress.

____ 20. I keep a stress journal to better understand and deal with things or people that cause me stress.

Section II (Manager)

To reduce my stress, I may delegate tasks to others. When I do:

____ 21. I make sure they see how the task is related to the value of the organization.

____ 22. I select the individual based on his or her ability and training needs.

____ 23. I try to assign a whole task rather than merely parts.

____ 24. I provide the necessary resources and authority to accomplish the task.

____ 25. I keep them informed as new information and resources come available.

____ 26. I specify the level of performance expected.

____ 27. I have the person agree on a schedule and deadline.

____ 28. I make sure that the person understands exactly what I want them to do.

____ 29. I follow up and maintain accountability for delegated tasks.

____ 30. I always thank them when they are finished.

____ 31. I identify the reason for the task and how it contributes to the group goals as well as to the individual's goals.

____ 32. I reward successful task completion.

____ 33. I don't constantly keep checking on progress.

____ 34. I invite feedback on how and to whom I delegate.

____ 35. I make sure the person is willing and able to accept the task.

Stress Assessment Analysis

This assessment is designed to help you discover your level of competency in handling stress so that you make improvements. The higher your scores, the better you are at dealing with stress.

You should encourage those in your group to consider changing their behavior on items for which their scores were either 3 or 4. You should strongly encourage them to change their behavior on items for which their score was only 1 or 2. Likewise, you should consider changing your behavior on items for which your scores are either 3 or 4, and you should definitely change your behavior on items for which your score was only 1 or 2.

Time Management Paradoxes

The Paradox of Our Time

We have taller buildings but shorter tempers, wider Freeways, but narrower viewpoints. We spend more but have less, we buy more, but enjoy less. We have bigger houses and smaller families, more conveniences, but less time.

The Performance Paradox

Organizations are able to maintain control by not knowing what exactly performance is.

Open-Door Paradox

Having a door open to improve communication may increase interruptions and distractions. "Open door" means "accessible," not a physically open door.

Planning Paradox

Failing to plan because of the time required results from failing to recognize that effective planning saves future time and achieves better results.

Crisis Paradox

Over-reacting to crises makes them worse.

Tyranny-of-the-Urgent Paradox

Responding to the urgent rather than the important neglects longer-term goals, which ensures future crises.

Meeting Paradox

Waiting for latecomers before starting meetings punishes punctuality and rewards tardiness. On the other hand, insisting on starting meetings at an exact time suggests inflexibility and over-emphasis on efficiency at the cost of effectiveness.

Delegation Paradox

Managers who do not delegate to inexperienced subordinates for lack of confidence in them perpetuate the problem by never giving subordinates a chance to learn and display competence through experience. A corollary is that delegating to those who are just as short of time as the manager may have long-term dysfunctional consequences.

Telephone Paradox

Insisting on talking with a boss instead of a secretary may delay getting information that is needed by the caller (also true for visits and interviews).

Long-Hours Paradox

The longer the hours a person works, the more fatigued and inefficient s/he becomes, so the longer it takes to complete tasks. A break and rest may do more to accomplish the task than putting in more time.

Activity Versus Results Paradox

Don't confuse activity with results. Don't concentrate on staying busy rather than on getting the right things done. When the objective becomes staying busy, people become "workaholics," a terrible illness.

Efficiency Versus Effectiveness

Managers may confuse efficiency with effectiveness and become more concerned about doing the job right than with doing the right job. No matter how efficient it is, if it is the wrong job, it will not be effective. A corollary is that devoting more and more time to doing the right short-term things neglects the costs associated with those accomplishments in the short-term as well as the foregone possible long-term objectives.

Paradox of Time

No one has enough time, but everyone has all there is.

Sources

Adapted from

Schwartz, E. B., & MacKenzie, R. A. (1977). Time management for women. *Management Review*, September, 19–25.

Meyer, M. W., and Gupta, V. (1994). The Performance Paradox. *Research in Organizational Behavior*(16), 309–369.

References

14 Cool Companies With Unlimited Vacation. (2018). Retrieved from https://www.glassdoor.com/blog/cool-companies-with-unlimited-vacation/

Albanese, R., & Van Fleet, D. D. (1985a). Free-riding: Theory, research, and implications. *Academy of Management Review, 10*(2), 244–255.

Albanese, R., & Van Fleet, D. D. (1985b). The free riding tendency in organizations. *Scandinavian Journal of Management Studies, 2*(2), 121–136.

Flint, D. (2018). *Think beyond value: Building strategy to win.* New York, NY: Morgan James.

Flint, G. D., & Van Fleet, D. D. (2011). The competitive cohort: An extension of strategic understanding. *Journal of Business Strategies, 28*(2), 97–122.

Gapp, R., Fisher, R., & Kobayashi, K. (2008). Implementing 5S within a Japanese context: An integrated management system. *Management Decision, 46*(4), 565–579.

Gerstel, N., & Clawson, D. (2918). Control over time: Employers, workers, and families shaping work schedules. *Annual Review of Sociology, 44*(1), 77–97.

Golden, L. (2003). Flexible work schedules and their impact on employees. In A. Sagie, S. Stashevsky, & M. Koslowsky (Eds.), *Misbehaviour and dysfunctional attitudes in organizations* (pp. 122–137). London, England. Palgrave Macmillan.

Graham, L. O. (1997). *Proversity.* New York, NY: Wiley.

Griffin, R. W., & Van Fleet, D. D. (2013). *Management skills: Assessment and development.* Mason, OH: SouthWestern.

Gutman, J. (1998). Means–end chains as goal hierarchies. *Psychology and Marketing, 14*(6), 545–560.

Quality Time, pages 91–92

Hirano, H. (1995). *5 pillars of the visual workplace.* Cambridge, MA: Productivity Press.

Kelly, E., & Moen, P. (2007). Rethinking the clockwork of work: Why schedule control may pay off. *Advances in Developing Human Resources, 9*(4), 487–506.

Kozlowski, S. W. J., & Bell, B. S. (2003). Work groups and teams in organizations. In W. C. Borman, D. R. Ilgen, & R. J. Klimoski (Eds.), *Handbook of psychology: Industrial and organizational psychology* (Vol. 12; pp. 333–375). New York, NY: Wiley-Blackwell.

Lin, C. S., Jeng, M. Y., & Yeh, T. M. (2018). The elderly perceived meanings and values of virtual reality leisure activities: A means-end chain approach. *International Journal of Environmental Research and Public Health, 15*(4), 663. https://doi.org/10.3390/ijerph15040663

Meyer, M. W., & Gupta, V. (1994). The performance paradox. *Research in Organizational Behavior,* (16), 309–369.

Morrison, R. N. (2017). *Activate human capital: A new attitude.* Bloomington, IN: Archway.

Polivka, A. E. (1996). Contingent and alternative work arrangements, defined. *Monthly Labor Review, 119*(10), 3–9.

Powell, G., & Mainiero, L. (2010). Managerial decision making regarding alternative work arrangements. *Journal of Occupational and Organizational Psychology, 72*(1), 41–56. https://doi.org/10.1348/096317999166482

Schwartz, E. B., & MacKenzie, R. A. (1977, September). Time management for women. *American Management Associations Management Review, 66*(9), 19–25.

Seeger, P. (2020, January). Retrieved from https://en.wikipedia.org/wiki/Keep_Your_Eyes_on_the_Prize

Stax Records. (1965). Retrieved from https://en.wikipedia.org/wiki/Respect_%28song%29.

Tedder, M. (2019, October 24). The 5-hour work day could transform the office — and make your life a whole lot better. *Money.* Retrieved from https://finance.yahoo.com/news/5-hour-day-could-transform-171152849.html

Van Fleet, D. D. (1982, August 13). Time-conscious bosses often focus more on the clock than the job being done. *Houston Chronicle,* Section 4: 3.

Van Fleet, D. D. (1986). Time: Quality vs. quantity. *InSite Magazine, 3*(9), 12–13.

Van Fleet, D. D., & Panevin, Y. L. (1992). Тайм-Менеджмент [Time-management]. Бизнес, (1992). 11–12.

Suggested Reading

Alexander, R. (1992). *Commonsense time management.* New York, NY: American Management Association.

Allen, J. E. (1986). *Beyond time management: Organizing the organization.* Reading, MA: Addison-Wesley.

Barkas, J. L. (1984). *Creative time management.* Englewood Cliffs, NJ: Prentice-Hall.

Bittel, L. R. (1991). *Right on time!: The complete guide for time pressured managers.* New York, NY: McGraw-Hill.

Black, R. (1987). *Getting things done: A radical new approach to managing time and achieving more at work.* London, England: Joseph.

Blyton, P. (1989). *Time, work, and organization.* London, England: Routledge.

Cory, K. D., Flint, G. D., & Van Fleet, D. D. (2013). V-REEL: An improved framework for teaching (and implementing) the resource-based view. *Journal of Strategic Management Education, 9*(1), 41–56.

Douglass, M. E., & Douglass, D. N. (1992). *Time management for teams.* New York, NY: American Management Association.

Ferner, J. D. (1980). *Successful time management.* New York, NY: Wiley.

Fontana, D. (1991). *Managing time.* New York, NY: Wiley-Blackwell.

Glew, D. J., O'Leary-Kelly, A. M., Griffin, R. W., & Van Fleet, D. D. (1995). Participation in organizations: A review of the issues and proposed framework for future analysis. *Journal of Management, 21*(3), 395–421.

Jenks, J. M., & Kelly, J. M. (1985). *Don't do. Delegate!* New York, NY: Ballantine Books.

Lakein, A. (1973). *How to get control of your time and your life.* New York, NY: Peter H. Wyden.

Quality Time, pages 93–95

Leana, C. R. (1987). Power relinquishment versus power sharing: Theoretical clarification and empirical comparison of delegation and participation. *Journal of Applied Psychology, 72*(2), 228–233.

LeBoeuf, M. (1979). *Working smart.* New York, NY: Warner Books.

Mackenzie, R. A. (1990a). *New time management methods for you and your staff.* Chicago, IL: Dartnell Corp.

Mackenzie, R. A. (1990b). *Teamwork through time management: New time management methods for everyone in your organization.* Chicago, IL: Dartnell.

MacKenzie, R. A. (1990c). *The time trap.* New York, NY: Amacom.

MacKenzie, R. A., & Waldo, K. C. (1981). *About time!* New York, NY: McGraw-Hill.

Mayer, J. J. (1993). *Winning the fight between you and your desk.* New York, NY: HarperBusiness.

McGeorge, D. (2018). *The 25 minute meeting: Half the time, double the impact.* Melbourne, Australia: Wiley.

McGeorge, D. (2019). *The first 2 hours: Make better use of your most valuable time.* Melbourne, Australia: Wiley.

Meier, G. S. (1983). *Worker learning and worktime flexibility.* Kalamazoo, MI: W. E. UpJohn Institute.

Oncken, W., Jr., & Wass, D. L. (1974). Management time: Who's got the monkey. *Harvard Business Review,* (November–December), 75–80.

Silcox, D., & Moore, M. E. (1980). *Woman time: Personal time management for women only.* New York, NY: Wyden Books.

Stokes, S. L., Jr. (1982). *It's about time.* Boston, MA: CBI.

Thomas, P. R. (1992). *Time warrior: Using total cycle time system to boost personal competitiveness.* New York, NY: McGraw-Hill.

Turla, P., & Hawkins, K. L. (1983). *Time management made easy.* New York, NY: E. P. Dutton.

Van Fleet, D. D. (1984, June 6). Talking on the job isn't waste of time. *USA Today.*

Van Fleet, D. D. (1985a, October 21–27). Free riders often costly to eliminate. *Dallas Times Herald.*

Van Fleet, D. D. (1985b). Handling free-riders. Personnel Report. *Research Institute of America,* (December), 6–7.

Van Fleet, D. D. (1985c). How to manage managerial time. *Oil Mill Gazetteer,* 14–17.

Van Fleet, D. D. (1985d, July). Business research. *Southwest Airlines Spirit,* 46.

Van Fleet, D. D. (1986). Time: Quality vs. quantity. *InSite Magazine, 3*(9), 12–13.

Van Fleet, D. D. (2017). Human capital, workplace violence, and human resource management in agribusiness: Review and recommendations. *Journal of Agribusiness, 35*(1), 53–74.

Van Fleet, D. D. (2018). Human capital and inappropriate behavior: Review and recommendations. *Journal of Human Resource and Sustainability Studies, 6*(4), 275–293.

Van Fleet, D. D., Flint, G. D., & Peterson, T. O. (2012). Participation, majority rule voting, and group cohesion. *Journal of Strategic Management Education, 8*(4), 54–68.

Van Ness, R. (1988). *Eliminating procrastination without putting it off.* Bloomington, IN: Phi Delta Kappa Educational Foundation.

Weeks, M. J., Heyel, C., & Lewis, D. V. (1989). *Taking control with time management* (3rd ed.). Boston, MA: American Management Association, Extension Institute.

Winston, S. (1983). *The organized executive: A program for productivity: New ways to manage time, paper, and people.* New York, NY: Norton.

About the Author

David D. Van Fleet is professor emeritus of management in the Morrison School of Agribusiness, W. P. Carey School of Business at Arizona State University. He is a past editor of both the *Journal of Management* and the *Journal of Behavioral and Applied Management.* He is or has been a member of the Board of Governors, Academy of Management, Southwest Federation of Academic Disciplines, and the Southern Management Association; and was national chair of the Management History Division of the Academy of Management. He is a fellow of both the Academy of Management and the Southern Management Association. He has been listed in Who's Who in the World, Who's Who in America, Who's Who Among America's Teachers, and Who's Who in Agriculture Academia. He has over 300 publications and presentations including 10 books (two with Information Age Publishing) and several websites for students. He has co-authored with colleagues from Poland, Russia, and Kuwait on topics related to managerial effectiveness in cross-cultural contexts. He has published in journals in Australia, Norway, Great Britain, Germany, and Russia as well as the United States. He has over 50 years of full-time teaching experience including 64 different courses.

Quality Time, page 97

Printed and bound by CPI Group (UK) Ltd, Croydon, CR0 4YY
18/09/2026
14964980-0001